Journeying with Jesus

By: Carole L. Haines

Volume 1

Hisshadowings

Devotionals

For more information, go to
https://HisShadowings.com

First paperback edition December 2020

Logo and Cover Design by: Cody J. Haines
for more information: https://www.namirostant.myportfolio

Cover Photo by: Anneliese Ott
for more: https://www.instagram.com/keyboardbrush/

ISBN: 978-1-7352596-6-6 Paperback
978-1-7352596-7-3. Digital

Published by:

Legacy Lane Publishing
Weatherford, TX
www.LegacyLanePublishing.com

Especially for You!

Thank you for your purchase.

Discover **more of Caroles' Writings**...and delight in a variety of **Bruce and Carole Haines' Inspirational Songs**,

Simply

1. **Scan** this QR Code

2. **Download** the free: **InSpireU App**

3. **Join** to access **even more Inspirational Works** from Heart-Centered Divinely Inspired Authors

4. **Input** This Special **Unlock Code:** **<u>800008</u>**

5. **Tap on** "Messengers" in the Side Menu Bar and **Find** **Carole L. Haines**

Another Special Gift

I try to spend time alone each morning with Jesus...and when I do, he gifts me with special messages, often in the form of poetry.

This **Book of Poems** is compiled from many of those precious messages He has bestowed upon me.

I hope you find as much comfort, enjoyment and healing in these messages as I have.

You can download your free copy here - http://bit.ly/Book-of-Poems .

Published by:

Legacy Lane Publishing

Weatherford, TX
303-242-4461

www.LegacyLanePublishing.com

TABLE OF CONTENTS

A Note from the Author

Sometimes, only suffering can produce beautiful things in our lives. The Apostle Paul shares this:

"From now on let no one cause trouble for me, for I bear on my body the brand marks of Jesus." (Galatians 6:17)

I bear literal scars of anxiety upon my body.

The Greek word which is translated as "Brand-marks "in the text, is ***stigma***, and figuratively means: "scars of service." I cried out to God many times in my life to take this struggle with anxiety away from me. He has not chosen to do so. But this anxiety has driven me to Him, to His Word, to my knees, and I am grateful for it. I would literally pick at my arms when worrying over matters, and it's left many scars. I was so embarrassed by these marks, until one day, God told me that I should not feel ashamed of them, that this anxiety disorder, that these scars are actually the birthmarks of His Love and Grace.

My anxiety drove me to seek someone I could fully trust and believe in. People have always failed me, but God never has. He has confused me in what

He has allowed to touch my life, but He has never, ever failed me.

How to Use This Book

Use this book as the Lord leads you. There is no formula in our walks with God. Your walk will be as unique as you are, let it be.

I encourage you to soak in one Devotion a day & meditate on the scripture God spoke to me the day I wrote it. I believe in the power of God's Word to transform a life and to make us whole from the inside out.

Sit long with His Word.

God testifies of His Word saying this,

"For My thoughts are not your thoughts,
Nor are your ways My ways," declares the Lord.
"For as the heavens are higher than the earth,
So are My ways higher than your ways
And My thoughts than your thoughts.
"For as the rain and the snow come down from heaven,
And do not return there without watering the earth
And making it bear and sprout,
And furnishing seed to the sower and bread to the eater;
So will My word be which goes forth from My mouth;
It will not return to Me empty, without accomplish-

ing what I desire,
And without succeeding in the matter for which I sent it.
(Isaiah 55:8-11 NASB)

Dedication

Dedicated to my precious Lord and Savior, Jesus Christ. He who is, who was, and who is to come.

I want to thank my husband, Bruce, for his encouragement in all my writing and all his time in listening to me read my blog posts to him beforehand. I love you, sweetheart. You are my treasure.

To my children, Derek, Meg, and Cody, you are such precious delights in my life. I could never have imagined such wonderful children. You are truly the joy of my heart.
May the Lord continue to guide you on your journey.

Be the Wonderful

For throughout all their journeys, the cloud of the Lord was on the tabernacle by day, and there was fire in it by night, in the sight of all the house of Israel. (Exodus 40:38)

I have wonderful people I get to spend my life with. I was dealing with some "hard things" happening and I began to whine a little about how hard life is. Let's face it, life is a struggle; it is hard, it can be wearying, just the daily-ness of it all. But as I was coming down from that "rant," I was reminded by God of something. Everyone's life is a struggle, some more than others, true, but no one gets through this life without a hassle.

I was reminded by God of just how wonderful my fellow strugglers are. I have the most precious husband any woman could ever have. I have three terrific adult children. I live in an old home, in a neighborhood that feels like a retreat center, deep in a lush, forested valley. I have so much to be thankful for, and my "rants" are a waste of time.

God challenged me to be the wonderful struggler for all of those around me who are struggling too. To come alongside them and struggle with them, as He does with us. We heard a sermon recently, entitled, "When things don't go according to plan." Ah, well, my life could be entitled, "Plan, what plan?" My life has never been one where things went smoothly. It seems to have been a Series of Unfortunate Events, to quote a famous book title; at least in the last ten years.

But I have the absolute most wonderful fellow strugglers walking alongside me in the midst of it all. And I have a God who tells me that He will work all things together for the good of those who love Him and know that they are called according to His purpose. God promises that He will accomplish all that concerns me. So even though my life has felt very random and unplanned, it is not my plans that matter, but His. So I challenge you today to "be the wonderful," in a fellow struggler's life. Be that person that they think of when life is just so hard. The one who brings a smile to their face and a sense of gratitude. When we choose to "be the wonderful," for others, we find that we have many, many wonderful people coming into our daily lives who are there for us through it all. And we are oh-so-thankful for them. God bless.

First Things First

This I recall to my mind, Therefore I have hope. The Lord's loving kindnesses indeed never cease, His compassions never fail. They are new every morning; Great is Your faithfulness. "The Lord is my portion," says my soul, "Therefore I have hope in Him." The Lord is good to those who wait for Him, To the person who seeks Him. It is good that he waits silently for the salvation of the Lord.

(Lamentations 3:21-26)

God asks me to be vulnerable a lot. God wants us to be transparent, genuine, honest with Him and with one another. No pretense, no games, no hiding behind masks. As I awoke this morning, so many things were vying for my attention. The dogs needed to go out, so out they went. But then, I was tempted to do a workout before my quiet time. I resisted. My mind then automatically drifted to the bank balance, "I wonder what it is? Did all those bills we paid hit yet?" and more. I resisted that too. I felt hungry. Distractions were popping up everywhere. But what all this showed me was that I sometimes forget to put first things first. If I claim that God is the most important person in my life, then my everyday choices will show it.

So, today, I made the best first choice. I chose

to sit with God before starting my day. There are days where I do not choose this, and truly, they can become chaotic. Yesterday was one of those days, and I never did get much of a sit-down with God. I missed Him very much. I mean, just look at God in the passage of Scripture above. Let's list them.

His loving kindnesses never cease, His compassions never, ever fail

His mercies are New every Morning

He is good to those who wait for Him,

He is my Portion

Every time I open the Word of God, I come to know Him better, and I come to see why I love Him so much. His love for me is boundless, unceasing, without measure. I fail Him too often, but He never fails me. I am blessed beyond my ability to express these blessings. There are no words full enough to declare His wonders. He is just the most beautiful person I have ever known. And yet I take God for granted almost every single day.

Forgive me, dearest Lord God Almighty. Your mercies are new every single morning. Teach me to bathe in them, to bask in the wonders of God. Everything else can wait. Help me to put first things first. You are my first, my best, and I love you. How can I possibly ever thank You enough for Your incredible love and faithfulness. Well, I can start by always choosing to be with You first every morning. Remind me to do this, teach me to wait upon You, dearest Lord. I love You, but more than that, your love inspires all I do. I sit here, awaiting Your words to me, and I am so excited to see You today. Amen.

Lose Control

Life is foggy, we can't see more than one step in front of us. A lot of times, we can't even see that next step. It's hard to be at peace without a sense of control over things. And yet, are we capable of controlling things at all?

O Lord, my heart is not proud, nor my eyes haughty; Nor do I involve myself in great matters, Or in things too difficult for me. Surely I have composed and quieted my soul; Like a weaned child rests against his mother, My soul is like a weaned child within me. O Israel, hope in the Lord From this time forth and forever.
(Psalm 131)

I have a friend who was following some people to a place, let's say a restaurant. She was in a completely unfamiliar area, back-woodsy and isolated. The next thing she knew, they had gotten too far ahead, and she felt lost. She panicked for a minute, thinking they weren't aware of her dropping back, but not too much time passed, and she found that they had pulled off, further up the road, and were waiting for her.

They hadn't forgotten her, they were waiting for her, to lead her and keep her safe. Her panic was all for nothing. But I tell you what: she will trust these people much more quickly in the future. Why? Because she was able to count on them in that situation. God allowed her to be in a situation that was completely out of her control, so that she could learn to trust these fellow believers just a little bit deeper, to take it to the next level, so to speak.

God, in His mercy, does this with us often. The desire for control is innate, inbred, natural. But it is not always good. It can become a habit, and once it's a habit, it can become an addiction. One of the hardest habits to break is the desire for control. Life feels so random sometimes. Nothing seems settled, reliable, steady, the ground seems to move beneath our feet. It is so hard not to just get in there and try to make things work out the way we think they should be.

Losing control, or our desire for control, is one of the hardest spiritual disciplines to master. We want God to show us all the blueprints. But if He did, we'd just try to build it ourselves. He wants a living, working, trusting relationship with us. He wants us to lose control and trust in Him.

The above Scripture is one that I pray often. One of the greatest lines in it says, "I do not involve myself in great matters, or in things too difficult for me." There's a balance to be struck between responsibility and control. Trusting God is the turn key in the door to that balance. The worst kind of control is when we try to control others. We manipulate, connive, scheme, and guilt trip people into doing what we want them to do. This is especially prevalent in marriages and in parenting. We try to control those we love or claim to love.

But is it really "loving" to control someone? Absolutely not. I have found that the root for all desire to control things in my own life is fear. And this particular kind of fear has to do with us feeling safe. Let's face it, relationships are risky, none of us wants to be betrayed, abandoned, or hurt. But manipulating others so that we can feel safe is just plain selfish. And, news flash, it doesn't work.

The only remedy for our fear and the need for safety is found in Psalm 131 above. To compose and quiet our souls, to rest in our Savior and Lord, to not involve ourselves in things that are too great for us. In other words—to trust God. The only way to trust anyone is to know them, to experience their faithfulness, like my friend earlier, who found that others were watching out for her. God is watching out for us. God is in control, our call is to lose control. We can trust Him on our road of life, He is watching over us...always.

The Unfolding of Your Word Gives Light

Your testimonies are wonderful; Therefore, my soul observes them. The unfolding of Your words gives light; It gives understanding to the simple.

Psalm 119:129

The unfolding of Your Word gives light. Oh, I just love that imagery. Like a flower unfolding, releasing its fragrance, God's Word unfolds before us in the midst of our darkness and gives us light. Life can be so confusing, so painful. So much happens that is completely out of our control. It is like a scary roller-coaster ride that we regret getting on sometimes.

But here we are, at the top of that hill, and there's no going back; we're going down again. When life gets like that, it's so good to know that God gives us His light in the midst of our darkness. This word unfolding means opening, entrance, doorway. God will create an opening out of the unknown, a doorway into His plans for us, an entrance into deep and wonderful places.

These places are full of light, grace, and encouragement. But we must sit with His Word, often and long, to have this "unfolding" happen. There is no quick in-and-out with God's Word. Yes, He will give us the needed words, rightly spoken, in times of need. But this unfolding comes with time spent with Him. So linger a little longer in His Word today, let Him unfold it before you and give you light. Let Him shine into some of those dark places in your life and bring you peace.

The Seemingly Insurmountable

Brethren, I do not regard myself as having laid hold of it yet; but one thing I do: forgetting what lies behind and reaching forward to what lies ahead, I press on toward the goal for the prize of the upward call of God in Christ Jesus. (Philippians 3:13-14)

I, like many others in our country, am trying to lose some extra weight, so I try to walk every day. I know that hills and stairs are good for me, so I try to pick places that have them. But I will tell you the truth, I hate them. Some people love them. They are the crazy ones I see running up the stairs and hills. But I approach the hills or stairs with dread, yet I ascend them nonetheless. I keep my head bowed and do not look up to see how far I have to go. I just look at the steps, and my feet, and take it one step at a time.

I think following God can be a lot like that. Keep our heads bowed, our eyes looking at our feet in humility, and just take it one step at a time. Some of the things God asks of us are seemingly insurmountable, but He promises to give us all we need. We can trust Him one step at a time.

The Lord makes firm the steps of the one who de-

lights in him; though he may stumble, he will not fall, for the Lord upholds him with his hand.
(Psalm 37:23-24)
Your word is a lamp to my feet and a light to my path. (Psalm 119:105)
You have also given me the shield of Your salvation, and Your help makes me great. You enlarge my steps under me, and my feet have not slipped.
(2 Samuel 22: 36-37)

We serve a God who promises that he will finish the work in us that He has begun. (Philippians 1:6) We can rest in His strength when we seem to be facing insurmountable changes, struggles and setbacks. Take heart and rest in His promises, He is faithful and good and will finish His work in each one of us.

Jesus the Example

Therefore, since we have so great a cloud of witnesses surrounding us, let us also lay aside every encumbrance and the sin which so easily entangles us, and let us run with endurance the race that is set before us, 2 fixing our eyes on Jesus, the author and perfecter of faith, who for the joy set before Him endured the cross, despising the shame, and has sat down at the right hand of the throne of God. For consider Him who has endured such hostility by sinners against Himself, so that you will not grow weary and lose heart.
(Hebrews 12:1–3)

There are things we must lay aside that encumber our journey with God. There are sins to be repented of that have entangled us, ensnared us. So let us put first things first, and deal with these. Only God has the right to cast our sins behind His back. We must come before Him, agree with Him about our sins, for that is what confession is, and turn and walk in His ways.
Brethren, I do not regard myself as having laid hold of it yet; but one thing I do: forgetting what lies behind and reaching forward to what lies ahead, I press on toward the goal for the prize of the up-

ward call of God in Christ Jesus. (Philippians 3:13-14)

In all of my life, one of the most important things I have learned is to deal with the past, and then put it behind you. 1 John 1:9 tells us that if we confess our sins, He is faithful to forgive us and to cleanse us from its unrighteousness. Part of that cleansing is from the guilt and shame.

So let us take these steps, one by one, fixing our eyes on Jesus, and reach forward to the upward call of God. His kingdom is here. His kingdom is coming. Let us do kingdom work until the very end. Let us be used up by God for good. Let us begin the ascent today; let's commit ourselves fully to Him for whatever His purposes are. Amen.

To Finish Well

Though your beginning was insignificant, Yet your end will increase greatly.
(Job 8:7)

Let's face it—most of life is a learning curve. How often have we all said or thought, "If only I knew then what I know now." Too often, the wears and cares of life can seep into our faith and make us sarcastic and cynical. We cease to trust God and one another. But God is bigger than all of life. I, too, have suffered greatly at the hands of others, both Christian and not.

I cannot tell you how often I have cried out to God to deliver me, to deliver our family, to vindicate us. My heart has soaked itself in the waters of disappointment, loss, and confusion. God never promised us that life will always go well, or make sense, or even be easy. Just recently, when sharing with a friend, God snuck in and awakened my heart to the fact that, as I've gotten older, I have desired life to get easier, instead of desiring Christ to be glorified.

My heart was cut to the quick, and I immediately began to cry. We both prayed and I repented of desiring a life of comfort and ease. Jesus never had an easy life. His life was filled with rejection, being slandered by mankind, and spoken of as a lunatic. He was constantly misunderstood, ceaselessly challenged, and continually sought after by people who just wanted to use Him. He was pursued by those who were always seeking a way to entrap Him with His own words.

He was surrounded by false accusers, arrogant liars, pleasers of men instead of pleasers of God. He got frustrated with them at times and let them know, in no uncertain terms, that He knew exactly who they were, who had sent them, and what their deceitful motives were. Our precious Lord was sought after constantly by people in need, people who were lost, people seeking a leader, a reason to live, a God of mercy. I love the verse I found this morning in Job:

Though your beginning was insignificant, Yet your end will increase greatly.
(Job 8:7)

I felt God speaking this directly to me this morning, and I turned it into a prayer. I asked God to use me up, to make my end increase greatly. I may have started small and been very insignificant;

but I desire to be used more intensely for the rest of my life. I desire to finish well. I don't want to slow down the pace for God now as I have gotten older. I don't want to retire from kingdom work, not now, not ever. I want to finish like the horse that comes from behind, in the "Run for the Roses," and takes the crown.

I take this crown only so I can prostrate myself before our precious Savior, and lay that crown before Him. Perhaps God has stirred your heart through this devotional this morning, as He has certainly stirred mine. Go to Him now, and tell Him that you want to finish well. Tell Him you desire the end of your life to be supercharged and powerful for the Kingdom of God. Join me in this desire to be used up by God. Amen and amen!

Being the Body of Christ

Today's Scripture passage is a long one. You might be tempted not to read the whole thing, but please, do read it! The jewels buried in this Scripture are life altering, especially in regard to being the Body of Christ.

But we prayed to our God, and because of them (our enemies' threats) we set up a guard against them day and night. Thus in Judah it was said, "The strength of the burden bearers is failing, Yet there is much rubbish; And we ourselves are unable To rebuild the wall... Our enemies said, "They will not know or see until we come among them, kill them and put a stop to the work." When the Jews who lived near them came and told us ten times, "They will come up against us from every place where you may turn, then I stationed men in the lowest parts of the space behind the wall, the exposed places, and I stationed the people in families with their swords, spears and bows...When I saw their fear, I rose and spoke to the nobles, the officials and the rest of the people: "Do not be afraid of them; remember the Lord who is great and awesome ,and fight for your brothers; your sons, your daughters, your wives and your houses." When our enemies heard that it was known to us, and that God had frustrated their plan, then all of us returned to the wall, each one to his work. From that day on, half of my servants carried on the work while half of them held the spears, the shields, the bows and the breastplates; and the captains were behind the whole house of Judah. Those who were rebuilding the wall and those who carried burdens took their load with one hand doing the work and the other holding a weapon... As for the builders, each wore his sword girded at his side as he built, while the trumpeter stood near me. I said to the nobles, the officials and the rest of the people, "The work is great and extensive, and we are separated on the wall far from one another. At whatever place you hear the sound of the trumpet, rally to us there. Our God will fight for us." So we carried on the work with half of them holding spears from dawn until the stars appeared. At that time I also said to the people, "Let each man with his servant spend the night within Jerusalem so that they may be a guard for us by night and a laborer by day." So neither I, my brothers, my servants, nor the men of the guard who followed me, none of us removed our clothes, each took his weapon even to the water. *(Nehemiah 4)*

Ever felt this way in your own life or as the Body of Christ? It's just too much, too big? I have. As a matter of fact, I'm feeling it right now. You know it's easier to trust God for the things we can't control, than the day-to-day things we face. Are we taking our armor out every day and protecting not only ourselves, but our fellow believers? Are we circling the wagons, or is it every man for himself? Wow!

Are we watching out for one another, protecting each other from the enemies that threaten to undo us, threaten to undo the work that God is doing in and through each of us, and all of us as a whole? I feel very alone in my struggles. Do you?

I need God to direct me in how to trust the Body of Christ, how to be the Body of Christ, and how to serve the Body of Christ. So I ask again, Are we being the Body of Christ, as described here in Nehemiah? I shall strive to change to become as such. Will you

A Time to Speak, Remain Silent, and Do the Work

So I came to Jerusalem and was there for three days. And I arose in the night, I and a few men with me. I did not tell anyone what my God was putting into my mind to do for Jerusalem and there was no animal with me except the animal on which I was riding. So I went out at night by the Valley Gate in the direction of the Dragon's Well and on to the Refuse Gate, inspecting the walls of Jerusalem which were broken down and its gates which were consumed by fire. Then I passed on to the Fountain Gate and the King's Pool, but there was no place for my mount to pass. So I went up at night by the ravine and inspected the wall. Then I entered the Valley Gate again and returned. The officials did not know where I had gone or what I had done; nor had I as yet told the Jews, the priests, the nobles, the officials or the rest who did the work. (Nehemiah 2:11–16)

God spoke to my heart about two and a half years ago to do something. I have prayed and been obedient to all the little steps He has asked me to take, but I told no one the big picture He had given me to carry out. Yesterday, during our pastor's sermon, I think God spoke to me again and restated His intentions for the work given to me two and a half years ago.

I am so overwhelmed by the task at hand. I have no idea how to do what He seems to be asking me to do. I need help; I can't do this on my own. So I shared with someone about it, and they told me someone else who may be able to help me walk this out. The time to speak had come.

I had prayed and obeyed behind the scenes, with no one really knowing, but now, I sensed God wanted me to speak to others about His Will for me. We do our best to hear from our precious God. Sometimes, we run ahead of Him; sometimes, we lag behind. But He is patient with us, spurring us on, rejoicing over each step we take toward Him. Just like a Mom and Dad rejoice over the little progressions their own children make, God rejoices over us.

There truly is a time to receive a vision or word from the Lord, and a time to pray about it. There is a time to be molded in silence, quietly becoming all we need to be for Him to work His wonders in and through us.

Then, there is a time to speak, a time to do what He has called, anointed, and equipped us to do.

I know that everything God does will remain forever; there is nothing to add to it and there is nothing to take from it, for God has so worked that men should fear Him. (Ecclesiastes 3:14)

Please pray for open doors and closed windows, as I navigate the course God seems to have set me on. Thanks.

Whatever you do, do your work heartily, as for the Lord rather than for men. (Colossians 3:23)

Heaps of Grace

"Go to sleep. It will all look better in the morning." Ever heard that? Sometimes, a day can go so wrong, things can seem so bad, and we've run out of time. It's late, we're tired, and we just can't make it alright before bedtime.

Perhaps we are powerless to make it right at all. Relationships can do that to us, because we have no control over another person's response or reaction. Circumstances can turn in an instant; in the blink of an eye, everything can change.

There are several incredibly wise, short and sweet, eye-opening little Scriptures tucked into the Word of God that are so incredibly practical. Let me show you a couple of them.

Also, do not take seriously all words which are spoken, so that you will not hear your servant cursing you. For you also have realized that you likewise have many times cursed others. (Ecclesiastes 7:22)

We don't really want to know those "secret things," people have said about us in the heat of the moment. We all get it wrong so many times, when we try to size up another person or a situation. This in no way excuses our outbursts, but it does call us to give grace to each other and to ourselves.

Remember, we've all gotten it wrong on countless occasions, like the above Scripture says, *"For you also have realized that you likewise have many times cursed others."*

But let us always strive to speak the truth in love to one another. Let's talk something out until we have come to resolution on a matter.

Let no unwholesome word proceed from your mouth, but only such word as is good for edification according to the need of the moment, so that it will give grace to those who hear. (Ephesians 4:29)

So what is an unwholesome word? I looked it up and it means, ***unhealthy, poisonous, something causing injury or ill-health.*** Pretty much anything that does not build someone up, but instead, tears them down.

I left the house after writing the beginning of the above post. God must have known that I was going to need this today. I ended up getting caught in the worst menagerie of detours imaginable. I was half an hour from where I needed to be, and ran into about a dozen traffic jams or detours.

About halfway through it, I just went off, I screamed an "unwholesome word" at the top of my lungs over and over, until I ran out of breath. I hit my steering wheel hard and screamed again. My twenty-one-year old son was sitting next to me, so I was really embarrassed when the barrage was over.

Did it feel good while I did it? Absolutely, it did! But it sure didn't feel good for my son.God tried to prepare me for the morning I would face, but I was not tuned into His voice.

Thank You, God, for trying to warn me about the terrible, awful morning I was about to have. Thank You for your incredible forgiveness and grace, which I need heaps of right now. Help me, and all of us reading this post today, to never be stingy with grace. You are certainly not. Help us to pour grace on ourselves and on others. Guide us to dance in Your fountain of grace and praise You for Your truly amazing love. I feel I am just beginning to understand and appreciate pure grace.

A Different Kind of Woe

Just watched what I think is one of the best films I have ever seen, and it's a true story. It's called ***The Prize Winner of Defiance, Ohio.*** It's a tale of triumph over potential tragedies, a tale of answered prayers, and second, third, and fourth chances.

It reminded me of how God is, at His deepest core, a Redeemer. He wastes not a single moment of our lives, but promises to work it all together for our good and His Glory. I was watching my friend who works with me, playing with one of our babies in the school. She rocked her back and forth and said, "Whoa, whoa, whoa," as the little one giggled and cheered. My mind picked up on the word whoa, and I realized there is another word that sounds exactly the same, but meaning something completely different.

Homophones are what we call these words in the world of linguistics, God is a redeemer. He turns our **woes** into **whoas**. He takes impossible situations and works them out. He takes what others consider worthless and makes something beautiful out of them. God is the originator of junk art.

We all, like sheep, have gone astray. Each of us has turned to our own way. But the Lord has caused the sin of us all to fall on Jesus (Isaiah 53:6).

He is the master craftsman. He sees the shattered lives and pieces them back together, more beautiful and stronger than they were originally. He is the potter and we are but clay. When we are hardened by sin or rebellion, He crushes us to powder, mixes us with living water of His Word, and makes a different, more beautiful, much more useful vessel out of us.

The word which came to Jeremiah from the Lord saying, "Arise and go down to the potter's house, and there I will announce My words to you." Then I went down to the potter's house, and there he was, making something on the wheel. But the vessel that he was making of clay was spoiled in the hand of the potter; so he remade it into another vessel, as it pleased the potter to make.

(Jeremiah 18:1-4)

Oh, the miraculous work of God. Each of us is that, a miraculous work of God. When we give our dysfunctions, our brokenness, our rebellion, our pride, our sins, etc. to God, He remakes us into masterpieces of His Grace. He takes our "woes" and gives us a different kind of “Whoa” instead.

Oh, the wonders of being a child of God, share the glory of His grace and kindness toward us with whomever He brings to you this day. Amen and amen.

While I Wasn't Looking

So I was waiting and watching for our bank deposit to happen. It usually happens at exactly the same time, but the clock was ticking...and nothing. I walked away for a while and came back, still nothing. I was getting pretty frustrated; I felt I needed this money right now, like yesterday would have been better. Things were tight, financially. I walked away and came back...still nothing.

I finally gave up for the night and went to sleep.
After all, I have to work in the morning. So I got up this morning, determined to spend time with God instead of checking my bank account one last time. I spent time in His Word, fellowshipping with Him instead of worrying. When I was done, I checked and it had happened. It happened while I wasn't looking. I was so worried about it, and it happened while I was asleep or fellowshipping with God..

The whole ordeal just shined a spotlight on how much I depend on worldly things, and not as much on God. It reminded me to go back to the basics of my faith.

For this reason I say to you, do not be worried about your life, as to what you will eat or what you will drink; nor for your body, as to what you will put on. Is not life more than food, and the body more than clothing? Look at the birds of the air, that they do not sow, nor reap nor gather into barns, and yet your heavenly Father feeds them. Are you not worth much more than they?
(Matthew 6:25–27)

God is constant, trustworthy, reliable. God is faithful, true, and dependable. God is always at work caring for me, for you, for all who trust in Him. I forget just how much I am worth to God. According to Jesus, I am certainly worth much more than the birds. My Heavenly Father feeds them and says, “Are you not worth much more than they?”

My Life on Backup

I have worked my first five-day week in quite a while, so it's been hard to write. But as I was straightening my house this morning and tidying up, I came across my backup memory for my laptop. I looked down at it and realized just how much of my writings are on it. All my poems, some of my journals, my songs, art, etc. It's a little plug-in device about three by five inches. I have been writing for about forty years now, so there's a lot of writing all around my house.

We just recently moved to a new home and stored some of the writings in the basement. Little did we know that the basement got wet whenever it rained, so all of those early writings of mine were ruined, lost forever. I even lost nine chapters of a book I started, but never finished, years ago. I started to grieve, but then remembered some Scriptures that lifted my spirits. Here they are:

I will cry to God Most High, To God who accomplishes all things for me. (Psalm 57:2)

The Lord will accomplish what concerns me; Your loving-kindness, O Lord, is everlasting; Do not forsake the works of Your hands. (Psalm 138:8)

Accomplishes...We usually have to write a list of our accomplishments on job resumes, or descriptions of ourselves for employment blurbs. But from a worldly perspective, my list of accomplishments is short. God doesn't keep the same kind of list that the world does. Jesus describes our list of accomplishments in a couple of verses:

"Teacher, which is the great commandment in the Law?" And He said to him, "You shall love the Lord your God with all your heart, and with all your soul, and with all your mind." This is the great and foremost commandment. The second is like it, "You shall love your neighbor as yourself." On these two commandments depend the whole Law and the Prophets.
(Matthew 22:36-39)

It's that simple, Love God and Love your neighbor. That is the main focus of our efforts in His Kingdom. That doesn't mean we don't talk about the hard stuff like, sin and hell. That would not be loving. But we must strive to speak all things in love, even as Jesus did.
Some thought Jesus was a homeless vagabond, born in a lowly stable, to a mother with a tainted reputation and what looked like a patched-up marriage.

But God was right there, working it all for their good, and for the good of all mankind, forever and ever. He is ever working in our lives too. Rest in His care, Dear Believer.

A God of Unity

Now may the God who gives perseverance and encouragement grant you to be of the same mind with one another according to Christ Jesus, so that with one accord you may with one voice glorify the God and Father of our Lord Jesus Christ. Therefore, accept one another, just as Christ also accepted us to the glory of God.

(Romans 15:5–7)

One of the greatest freedoms we experience as Americans is freedom of

______________________________. You fill in the blank. The freedoms we are granted here in this country are unprecedented. But there is a freedom that cannot be granted by anyone but God Himself. It is the freedom of unity. We are so into celebrating individuality here in America, we seem to have forgotten the beauty of unity. But unity has been experienced in this country in times of war.

Tom Brokaw called a generation The Greatest, in his book. I believe he is right in so many ways. The acts of sacrifice and community that were seen during this tragic, yet triumphant time of war were both beautiful and astounding.

Brothers and sisters, we are in a time of great trial as believers in Jesus Christ. But our struggle is not with other people. For our struggle is not against flesh and blood, but against the rulers, against the powers, against the world forces of this darkness, against the spiritual forces of wickedness in the heavenly places.

(Ephesians. 6:12)

God has granted us the miraculous power to be of one mind, to be of one accord, to glorify Him with one voice. Let us pull together, lay aside our petty differences, and fulfill the call of Christ, to reach a world in need of His saving love and grace. Let us only have as important to us that which is important to Christ and Him alone.

Nothing else really matters. None of our petty disagreements are ever going to matter in heaven, so let us lay them aside down here, and live for Christ alone. He is the author and perfecter of not only our faith, but also of our unity. Let us yield to His marvelous grace and live out the freedom of being of one mind, in one accord, and glorifying God with one voice. Oh, then the world shall see Jesus. They shall see Jesus in us.

Having Been with Jesus

Now as they observed the confidence of Peter and John and understood that they were uneducated and untrained men, they were amazed, and began to recognize them as having been with Jesus. (Acts 4:13)

Could there ever be a higher compliment given to any of us? They began to recognize them as having been with Jesus.

Oh, Father God, we pray that as people observe us, listen to us, and see how we live our lives, they would begin to recognize us as having been with Jesus. I pray that as people observe me, as they did Peter and John, and understand that I am an uneducated and untrained woman, may they be amazed at what You, Jesus, can do in a life that is surrendered, a life that is yielded. You have completely changed my world, Jesus.

I thought my life was ruined, but You stepped in and took this ruined life and made me completely whole. You took the brokenness, the loneliness, the loss, the instability, the anxiety, the confusion, the pain. You took it all, bore it all, redeemed it all.

You truly are the *God who gives life to the dead and calls into being that which does not exist* (Romans 4:17).

I praise You, dearest Father, Savior Jesus, and precious Holy Spirit. The greatest thing that could ever be said about me, is that "I can tell, she has been with Jesus." Make it so, dearest Lord, not just in me, but in all who follow You.

Legacies

What example are we passing on to the next generation of believers in the Body of Christ? Are we overcomers or quitters? Do we endure hardships, persecutions, failures, disappointments, and yet still press on toward the upward call of God in Christ Jesus?

Not that I have already obtained it or have already become perfect, but I press on so that I may lay hold of that for which also I was laid hold of by Christ Jesus. Brethren, I do not regard myself as having laid hold of it yet; but one thing I do: forgetting what lies behind and reaching forward to what lies ahead, I press on toward the goal for the prize of the upward call of God in Christ Jesus.
(Philippians 3:13-14)

Let us not grow weary in doing good, no matter what obstacles we face, no matter what offenses we must endure, no matter who comes against us. Let us endure and join the ranks of the overcomers. For if God is for us, who can be against us?

Let us leave legacies of grace and kindness, legacies of strength and endurance, legacies of love and faith. Let us leave the legacy of overcomers, for those who are coming up behind us, those who are watching how we handle life. To God be the glory.

But They Cried Out All The More

As they were leaving Jericho, a large crowd followed Him. And two blind men sitting by the road, hearing that Jesus was passing by, cried out, "Lord, have mercy on us, Son of David!" The crowd sternly told them to be quiet, but they cried out all the more, "Lord, Son of David, have mercy on us!" And Jesus stopped and called them, and said, "What do you want Me to do for you?" They said to Him, "Lord, we want our eyes to be opened." Moved with compassion, Jesus touched their eyes; and immediately they regained their sight and followed Him. (Matthew 20:29-34)

I was struck by many things in this little gem of a story. *First*, these men were not intimidated by the large crowd around Jesus. Those who have lost one of their senses have been found to have even keener senses in those that remain. Blind people tend to hear much better than the seeing do, so I know these men heard the large crowd following Jesus, but they cried out to Him anyway. And when the crowd tried to hush them up, it says, "but they cried out all the more." I think we give up on issues in prayer far too easily, I know I do.

I have several things that I am praying about

right now, and they are far beyond my ability to do anything about them, so I pray hard. I am learning to just ask and keep on asking. The other thing I noticed was Jesus response to these men, "And Jesus stopped and called them, and said, 'What do you want Me to do for you?'" I am learning to be very specific in my prayers and in my crying out to God. I am learning to trust Him in childlike faith.

O Lord, my heart is not proud, nor my eyes haughty; Nor do I involve myself in great matters, Or in things too difficult for me. Surely I have composed and quieted my soul; Like a weaned child rests against his mother, My soul is like a weaned child within me. O Carole, hope in the Lord From this time forth and forever. (Psalm 131)

Notice how I placed my own name in the Psalm. I pray Scripture over people and situations all the time. I feel so weak and I want to do so much, but I am so limited. I've discovered that God didn't just give me my gifts and talents, he also gave me my limitations and boundaries. He has a sovereign purpose for both.

I am learning to live within those boundaries with great victory and great peace. These blind men had learned to live with their weakness, but they wanted to be whole, they didn't give up on their desire to be healed. When Jesus was passing by, they cried out to Him, and He asked them what they wanted. They told Jesus, "Lord, we want our eyes to be opened." Notice the "we" in their request. They were not just concerned with themselves, but with each other. They had grown to care for one another in their weakness. They depended on each other, they trusted each other.

Oh, Body of Christ, how much we can learn from the humility and tenacity of these two men. Let us come to Jesus, as little children, as Psalm 131 teaches us, with childlike trust and faith. Let us just lay our heavy burdens at His feet cry out all the more. Let us not grow weary in our prayers about the things in our lives and in the lives of those around us. Jesus is always passing by, He is always listening. He is our precious Savior and He is so good and gracious, merciful and kind. Let us say with the Psalmist: *"O______________________________, hope in the Lord. From this time forth and forever." You fill in the blank with your own name*. He is listening. Just ask, and keep on asking.

Concerning the Word of Life

What was from the beginning, what we have heard, what we have seen with our eyes, what we have looked at and touched with our hands, concerning the Word of Life—and the life was manifested, and we have seen and testify and proclaim to you the eternal life, which was with the Father and was manifested to us—what we have seen and heard we proclaim to you also, so that you too may have fellowship with us; and indeed our fellowship is with the Father, and with His Son Jesus Christ. These things we write, so that our joy may be made complete.

(1 John 1:1-4)

Our relationship with God through Jesus Christ must be experienced through all the five senses. It is not just an intellectual exercise through the Word of God. It is something we carry with us each day into our jobs, out into the world, in our own homes. What was from the beginning, what we have ***heard***, what we have ***seen*** with our eyes, what we have looked at and touched with our hands, concerning the Word of Life.

We share what God reveals to us in His Word. We encourage others with what He shows us from

His Word and how it impacts our everyday lives. We tell of what He has shown us, even as the heavens declare the glory of God. All around us are His wonders. Within us, we carry the miraculous...a redeemed life. Saved from the downward spiral of the destructive nature of sin and failure, the repetitive cycle we were once doomed to live in.

"And the life was manifested, and we have seen and testify and proclaim to you the eternal life, which was with the Father and was manifested to us." (Verse 2).

We share how the word of life has changed everything for us, inside and out. Manifested, lived out...right in front of all who care to take notice of the changes Jesus brings. Jesus is our manifesto. He is the firstborn from among the dead. We were all once dead in our trespasses and sins, but God has made us alive through Christ. Oh, shout hallelujah!

"What we have seen and heard we proclaim to you also, so that you too may have fellowship with us; and indeed our fellowship is with the Father, and with His Son Jesus Christ." (Verse 3).

A walk with Jesus Christ is so eye-opening, so refreshing, so real and poignant, it practically demands to be shared. We cannot help but tell others the difference He is making in our lives. "I once was lost, but now I'm found." I used to not belong anywhere. But Jesus is now my home, my hope, my all.

"These things we write, so that our joy may be made complete." (Verse 4). Notice how it says here that "we write these things so that our own joy is made complete."

I was feeling discouraged about this blog and wondering if I should continue writing these devotionals. I asked God to give me a sense, a sign of whether I should continue. I never know who reads them, or if they are reaching people. But then God showed me that I write these things so that my own joy is made complete. I must share what He has done for me, and this is one of the ways He has shown me to do this.

May God bless all and any who read this today. Share your own experiences with Jesus Christ. Visit my website at hisshadowings.com. I would love to hear how He is working in your own life.

Otherworldly

But get up and stand on your feet; for this purpose I have appeared to you, to appoint you a minister and a witness not only to the things which you have seen, but also to the things in which I will appear to you; rescuing you from the Jewish people and from the Gentiles, to whom I am sending you, to open their eyes so that they may turn from darkness to light and from the dominion of Satan to God, that they may receive forgiveness of sins and an inheritance among those who have been sanctified by faith in Me.
(Acts 26:16–18)

Otherworldly is the only word I can think of to describe what my husband and I, along with a team of a couple dozen other people, just experienced. We traveled to another country to participate in outreach and sharing the good news Of Jesus Christ with those from a completely different culture than our own. You can't get more different than this foreign land is from the USA, and yet we had so much in common with our brothers and sisters in Christ who lived and ministered there.

There is a bond that Jesus creates among His People that cannot be matched anywhere else. I've always felt small and little, as if I did not have much to offer to God for His purposes. But I gave God all I am, all I had; as insignificant as it all is, and He did a mighty work through all of us. `

I watched a team of extremely different people pull together and accomplish a monumental task. They traveled great distances, and reached out to those who have been crying out to God and seeking Him with all their hearts.

We shared the road with cows, stray dogs, pedestrians, cyclists, rickshaws, three-wheeled taxis, buses, trucks, and cars. The noise sounded throughout the city from about 6:00 a.m. to midnight. One of the most unique were the car horns.

But when we reached our little remote villages, the joy on the people's faces cannot ever be described in words. These precious and beautiful people love Jesus so very much and desire to reach their own people for Him. There are just no words to describe the treasure that these people are to me now. Each one is a precious jewel in the crown of Jesus.

So, yes, I am so glad to be home again to what is familiar to me. But my life is now forever changed because I have gone, seen, been a part of, and touched brothers and sisters in Christ in another land. I feel like I had a taste of Heaven and experienced God's promises firsthand like never before.

After these things I looked, and behold, a great multitude which no one could count, from every nation and all tribes and peoples and tongues, standing before the throne and before the Lamb, clothed in white robes, and palm branches were in their hands; and they cry out with a loud voice, saying, "Salvation to our God who sits on the throne, and to the Lamb." (Revelation 7:8-10)

For me now, and all who have ever worshipped with believers from another culture or land, Heaven has already begun. Thank You, God.

His Trembling Flame

The wind of the Spirit passes through us igniting our passions for Christ. We quiver and shake as we become whoHe envisioned us to be before the foundation of the world. We're His Trembling Flame with whispers of hope spoken through us, to a world that is languishing here in the dark. Where once there lay nothing but wasteland our Lord uses us as His spark. Where all is dried out and withered, where Living water has never brought life; it is there that our Lord God will send us and use us as His Trembling Flame.

Fear not dear believer when you feel afraid for when we are weak He is strong, just move forward in faith, stepping out is His name and become, where you are, a part of the Fire, another spark of His Trembling Flame. When the day of Pentecost had come, they were all together in one place. And suddenly there came from heaven a noise like a violent rushing wind, and it filled the whole house where they were sitting. And there appeared to them tongues as of fire distributing themselves, and they rested on each one of them. And they were all filled with the Holy Spirit and began to speak with other tongues, as the Spirit was giving them utterance. (Acts 2:1-4)

Let Your Story Become His-Story

We are drowning in our own history. We have often heard that if we don't learn from history, we are doomed to repeat it. This can be very true, and it is never more true than when we are tangled in a web of unforgiveness.

I have seen people so determined to bleed every last drop of blood out of a situation that has gone wrong.

"Well, they owe me an apology!" or perhaps,

"Well, they started it."

Have you been there? I have, and I can tell you that there is no way to make things right on a human level. I believe this is why God says,

"Never take your own revenge, beloved, but leave room for the wrath of God, for it is written, 'Vengeance is Mine, I will repay,' says the Lord." (Romans 12:19).

We forget that we are powerless to affect change in anyone but ourselves. And the only true way to affect change in ourselves is to give ourselves to God. He is our Creator, our sustainer, our

Savior.

"And we know that God causes all things to work together for good to those who love God, to those who are called according to His purpose." (Romans 8:28)

We see in this verse that it is God who can work it all for good, not us. We are called to believe that God loves us, and that He has a purpose for our lives, even all the pain. So, let go of all those things others have done to you.

Give these things into the hands of the only one who can do something about them, God. Give God your history and let Him make it into His-Story. I have done this, and the freedom that I now walk in is absolutely unparalleled. He is truly able to work all things together for good. My story of loss, ruin, hurt, betrayal, brokenness, and strife have been and continue to be rewritten in His-Story.

Give Your life to the one who made You, and watch Him work His wonders. Go from drowning to soaring. It's a long journey, but it is so incredibly freeing.

Just Say the Word

When Jesus returned to Capernaum, a Roman officer came and pleaded with him, "Lord, my young servant lies in bed, paralyzed and in terrible pain." Jesus said, "I will come and heal him." But the officer said, "Lord, I am not worthy to have you come into my home. Just say the word from where you are, and my servant will be healed. I know this because I am under the authority of my superior officers, and I have authority over my soldiers. I only need to say, 'Go,' and they go, or 'Come,' and they come. And if I say to my slaves, 'Do this,' they do it." When Jesus heard this, he was amazed. Turning to those who were following him, he said, "I tell you the truth, I haven't seen faith like this in all Israel! And I tell you this, that many Gentiles will come from all over the world—from east and west—and sit down with Abraham, Isaac, and Jacob at the feast in the Kingdom of Heaven." (Matthew 8:5-11 NLT)

Dearest Jesus, I need faith like this. My faith is so "circumstantial" sometimes. You are the same yesterday, today, and forever; but I am nowhere near that reliable. You have poured Yourself into my heart through faith in You. All the faith, all the joy, all the peace and mercy—it's already in there. Through the power of Your Holy Spirit, guide me to get out of the way, so that more of You can come through me. You have never, ever failed to lead me, and You never will. Thank You, Jesus, dearest king of my life. Continue to teach me to decrease, so that more and more of You shines through more and more of me. Amen.

I Am Living Proof

I love the Lord, because He hears my voice and my supplications. Because He has inclined His ear to me, Therefore I shall call upon Him as long as I live. The cords of death encompassed me and the terrors of Sheol came upon me; I found distress and sorrow. Then I called upon the name of the Lord: "O Lord, I beseech You, save my life!" Gracious is the Lord, and righteous; Yes, our God is compassionate. The Lord preserves the simple; I was brought low, and He saved me. Return to your rest, O my soul, For the Lord has dealt bountifully with you. For You have rescued my soul from death, My eyes from tears, my feet from stumbling. I shall walk before the Lord in the land of the living. I believed when I said, "I am greatly afflicted."
I said in my alarm, "All men are liars." What shall I render to the Lord for all His benefits toward me? I shall lift up the cup of salvation and call upon the name of the Lord. I shall pay my vows to the Lord, Oh may it be in the presence of all His people. Precious in the sight of the Lord is the death of His godly ones. O Lord, surely I am Your servant, I am Your servant, the son of Your handmaid, You have loosed my bonds. To You I shall offer a sacrifice of

thanksgiving, and call upon the name of the Lord. I shall pay my vows to the Lord, Oh may it be in the presence of all His people, In the courts of the Lord's house, In the midst of you, O Jerusalem. Praise the Lord!
(Psalm 116)

This Psalm reads like my very own testimony. I don't need to add any words to it. Our precious God is compassionate beyond measure. He truly works all things together for good.
A Precious friend often says, "Hang around for the rest of the story." All I can say is, if you are despairing right now, if you are suffering and wrestling with thoughts of desperation. Please give your life over to God through faith in His Son, Jesus Christ.

He really does work all things together for good. He really does bring beauty from the ashes of our ruined lives. He truly is the God of second chances. He is truly the God who *gives life to the dead and calls into being that which does not exist.*
(Romans 4:17)
I am living proof.

Apples of Gold

Like apples of gold in settings of silver is a word spoken in right circumstances. (Proverbs 25:11)
When they bring you before the synagogues and the rulers and the authorities, do not worry about how or what you are to speak in your defense, or what you are to say; for the Holy Spirit will teach you in that very hour what you ought to say. (Luke 12:11–12)

Things can get dicey out there in this world. We find ourselves in circumstances not of our own choosing. It reminds me of what Frodo said to Gandalf in *"Lord of the Rings,"* J.R.R Tolkien.
Frodo: *I wish the ring had never come to me. I wish none of this had happened.*
Gandalf: *So do all who live to see such times. But that is not for them to decide. All we have to decide is what to do with the time that is given to us. There are other forces at work in this world Frodo, besides the will of evil. Bilbo was meant to find the Ring. In which case, you were also meant to have it. And that is an encouraging thought.*

In this world of intrigue and uncertainty, we have a God who will give us the words to speak that will encourage others and strengthen ourselves. So often, we don't wait on Him, we don't ask Him what He would have us do. We just react to situations and circumstances.

That is what I did yesterday. I just reacted to an unforeseen circumstance. I'm sure you all can understand that one of the easiest places to lose your cool is when driving, especially when you are already frustrated about something else. I wasn't prepared because I was whining and complaining about something else that went wrong, and then—boom—I reacted badly to another person's bad behavior. It's that quick.

I know My Lord has forgiven me, I asked Him to, and He promised that "*if we confess our sins, He is faithful and just to forgive us our sins and to cleanse us from all unrighteousness.*" (1 John 1:9).

But I say all this to encourage each of us to spend lots of time alone with God, for in these times, He is preparing us to actively respond in His way to unforeseen circumstances and situations. When we learn to wait on Him and keep our eyes fixed on Jesus, then we too shall find ourselves speaking right words, like "*apples of gold in settings of silver.*"

Precious, in Life and in Death

"I love You, O Lord, my strength." The Lord is my rock and my fortress and my deliverer, My God, my rock, in whom I take refuge; My shield and the horn of my salvation, my stronghold. I call upon the Lord, who is worthy to be praised, And I am saved from my enemies. The cords of death encompassed me, and the torrents of ungodliness terrified me. The cords of Sheol surrounded me; the snares of death confronted me. In my distress I called upon the Lord, and cried to my God for help; He heard my voice out of His temple, and my cry for help before Him came into His ears. (Psalm 18:1-6)

Ninety-degree temperatures are beginning to smolder the gardens I have worked so hard on this spring. I slipped out my front door at around 6:00 a.m. this morning to give my precious flowers a much needed drink. As I was showering these beauties, my eyes caught sight of something shivering in the grass. I put down the hose and went over to find a beautiful luna moth shivering, shaking. Thankfully, I had not watered this precious little creature, but I suspect one of my cats had captured it in the night.

There was a large tear in one of its wings, and I could tell this little guy was in rough shape. I picked it up, placed it in a safe place, as my son grabbed our large dog carrier. He lined it with gentle leaves and one large branch to sit on. I put in a tiny water dish. I placed the little creature in the dog carrier, knowing it would probably die, but at least it would die in peace. I marveled at the beauty and grace of this intricately decorated moth.

This whole scene reminded me of how God gingerly cradles us when we are feeling so fragile. As the above Scripture says, when we call on God in our distress, and pray for help from heaven; He hears us. He answers us and comes and gives us Himself, His presence.

Perhaps He doesn't answer the way we'd like, but He cradles us, protects us, watches over us and brings us through. What a precious, tender and loving God we have.

Let us rest in His care.

"Precious in the sight of the Lord is the death of His Godly Ones." (Psalm 116:15).

What we suffer at times, can feel like a type of death, and God cradles us as He brings us through to the other side. Whether we live or die, His presence amidst all that life can throw at us is His greatest gift.

Journeying to Him

But if we walk in the Light as He Himself is in the Light, we have fellowship with one another, and the blood of Jesus His Son cleanses us from all sin. If we say that we have no sin, we are deceiving ourselves and the truth is not in us. If we confess our sins, He is faithful and righteous to forgive us our sins and to cleanse us from all unrighteousness.
(1 John 1:7-9)

Here we go again, another place of fresh starts, another struggle I must overcome, another loss redeemed. So I sit here at the feet of the Only One who has ever conquered death and shame .The Only One who can save me by the Power of His Name.

Jesus, I find myself again, Journeying to You. Holding in my hand this same failure, this same place, this same need. I am trusting that You are not tired of empowering me, strengthening me to begin again this journey I have so many times failed to finish.

Perhaps I've failed because I could not see that I am not alone and I am not forsaken, I am not defeated. Fallen, Yes, scuffed knees, bleeding sores, bruised ego, Yes. But defeated, absolutely not, because You, Jesus, have overcome the world. I can too, overcome the world, in You, Jesus, in Your strength.

So I find myself again, Journeying to You and giving You what I have failed at once more. Seeking You to be Powerful in me, so that I may stand on Victor's shore and look out over the vast ocean which is My life with You.

I need never look back, for You have forgotten my sin. My freedom cost You so much. But You freely gave and You freely call my name. You invite us to come begin our Journeying with You once again.

Scan the Code Above to Listen to "Listening to God"...Composer Songwriter: Bruce Haines. Sung by: Carole L Haines & Bruce Haines.

(Direct Link: https://soundcloud.com/hisshadowings/listening-to-god)

Fellow Workers

For even as the body is one and yet has many members, and all the members of the body, though they are many, are one body, so also is Christ. For by one Spirit we were all baptized into one body, whether Jews or Greeks, whether slaves or free, and we were all made to drink of one Spirit. For the body is not one member, but many. If the foot says, "Because I am not a hand, I am not a part of the body," it is not for this reason any the less a part of the body.
(1 Corinthians 12:12–15)

I was hoping for some peace and quiet on this long-awaited spring morning. The sun was shining, the birds were chirping outside, and then reooowww, reow, ruuummm! The sound of chainsaws burst forth from the driveway down the road.

At first I was annoyed, then a bit jealous, wishing that I had lined them up to trim some of my overhanging branches. I went out on the porch stoop, cup of morning coffee in hand, and just watched.

I observed several workers, each doing a different job. One was on the ground, pulling the smaller branches out of the way as they were cut from above. another was precariously hovering over the large tree in a cherry picker, cutting branches from above, first the smaller ones, then the larger limbs. Our third man was obviously the supervisor. I discerned this because he was orchestrating everything going on, both on the ground and up above. He was making sure the worker below was safe from the falling branches, and that the worker in the tree was safe in his perch.

It was quite wonderful to watch. They worked so well as a team. What if the man in the tree had neglected to watch out for his worker below? What if the worker below refused to move the branches and put them in the wood-chipper? What if the supervisor had gone away to get coffee, leaving the crew in a dangerous position? They all had their places, did their tasks, watched out for one another.

When we are working alone in the Body of Christ, we watch out for and care for our fellow workers. All the jobs are equally important. All are very necessary. Some may be more upfront or visible, but all are important to God.

Let us value, protect, and encourage one another. We are members of one another.(God sees and He loves us each the same. There is a precious wonder in watching God accomplish His Will through people who work together, with all their different gifts interlocking into a beautiful creation.

Rejoice, O Members of His Body and delight in where He has placed you. We need you, I need You. God loves us all. Let's bring Him joy this day.

Anticipating Blooms

I was just outside, watering my garden. Every year, I take one of those huge packs of wildflower seeds and I spread them along this one long part of my garden. I water them into the ground, over and over again, and wait and watch to see what will come up. I love doing this so much. So far, I have pretty pink cosmos, Black-eyed Susans, shasta daisies, poppies, and one or two others I don't know the names for.

There is one plant in particular I can't wait to see bloom. I have never had this foliage show up in one of the seed packs before, so I'm chomping at the bit, anticipating the day when I will get to see these flowers. They are currently in the bud stage, so I won't have to wait long to see just what these beauties will be.

Walking with God is a bit like that. We can see Him working His wonders in our own lives and in the lives of other people all around us. We watch as He weaves His beautiful tapestry throughout the canvas of our lives. Sometimes we recognize what He is doing, other times we are excitedly waiting, watching Him work, wondering when we will see those long-anticipated blooms appear. And we will rejoice with Him in His work.

I love God and how He works wonders in the universe, in us, and in the lives of people all around us. I love how He uses us to accomplish great and mighty things we could never have imagined in our own minds.

(Read Ephesians 1:3-12)

The Mystery of Prayer

While He was still speaking, they came from the house of the synagogue official, saying, "Your daughter has died; why trouble the Teacher anymore?" But Jesus, overhearing what was being spoken, said to the synagogue official, "Do not be afraid any longer, only believe." And He allowed no one to accompany Him, except Peter and James and John the brother of James. They came to the house of the synagogue official; and He saw a commotion, and people loudly weeping and wailing. And entering in, He said to them, "Why make a commotion and weep? The child has not died, but is asleep." They began laughing at Him. But putting them all out, He took along the child's father and mother and His own companions, and entered the room where the child was. Taking the child by the hand, He said to her, "Talitha kum!" (which translated means, "Little girl, I say to you, get up!"). Immediately the girl got up and began to walk, for she was twelve years old. And immediately they were completely astounded. And He gave them strict orders that no one should know about this, and He said that something should be given to her to eat.

(Mark 5:35-43)

I am going to take you on a slightly different journey with this story. It is so hard to keep praying for those we love who do not know Jesus yet. It seems we pray so long and hard. Sometimes, we lose hope, and stop praying. This happened to me, and I will never forget that while I was at Bible Study one morning, God whispered to me, “Don’t give up on her!” It was as clear as a bell, not audible, but clear.

Has anybody else out there ever struggled like this, with praying for lost loved ones, as I have? I have often shared this verse with others. It is one of my mainstays. *“So will My word be which goes forth from My mouth; It will not return to Me empty, without accomplishing what I desire, And without succeeding in the matter for which I sent it.”* (Isaiah 55:11).

I have done all I know to do for my loved ones. I have taught them the Word. I have prayed, and still pray for them. I have sought to love them as Christ loves me. I have served them, asked their forgiveness when I’ve been wrong. Yet, some are still not walking with Him.

My heart has ached with longing for them to come and know this glorious God through Jesus Christ. And still I wait.

But I comfort myself and I strengthen myself, feeding on the promises of God's Word. God is outside of time, not bound by it, not imprisoned to it, and certainly not measuring progress by it.
Man looks at the outward appearance, but God looks at the heart. (1 Samuel 16:7).

As I was reading the story above of Jairus's daughter, who had died, I was reminded of my loved ones who need Jesus. Some received them as children, but have slipped away. Some have never known Jesus before. All I know is that God told me not to give up on them, and He whispered to me this morning, "Remember that I am the God who gives life to the dead, even those who seem spiritually dead."

So even if I feel discouraged, I will not give up, while there is still breath in me. He loves our loved ones more than we ever could. So let's keep on praying. Let's keep on believing God for His great and precious promises.

But God

Therefore, having been justified by faith, we have peace with God through our Lord Jesus Christ, through whom also we have obtained our introduction by faith into this grace in which we stand; and we exult in hope of the glory of God. And not only this, but we also exult in our tribulations, knowing that tribulation brings about perseverance; and perseverance, proven character; and proven character, hope; and hope does not disappoint, because the love of God has been poured out within our hearts through the Holy Spirit who was given to us. (Romans 5:1-5)

I once was separated from God, alone and orphaned, wandering aimlessly in my spirit, and finding no rest.

But God—don't you just love that phrase: ***but God***. It's a game changer for all of us who believe in Him.

Having been justified by faith - past tense.

We have peace with God - present tense.

And Hope does not disappoint - future tense.

Truly, He has enclosed me behind and before and has laid His hand upon me. Such knowledge is too wonderful for me. It is too high for me to understand. (Psalm 139:5-6).

And yet, there it is, and here we are, standing in grace, His undeserved favor. The Apostle Paul called himself the chief of sinners. I have found that the closer we come to Jesus, the more aware we become of our failings. Even so, we become more aware of just how far-reaching His grace is. Grace that forgives and covers those sins.

Therefore we do not lose heart, but though our outer man is decaying, yet our inner man is being renewed day by day. For momentary, light affliction is producing for us an eternal weight of glory far beyond all comparison, while we look not at the things which are seen, but at the things which are not seen; for the things which are seen are temporal, but the things which are not seen are eternal. (2 Corinthians 4:16–18)

I love how it says, *"While we look not at the things which are seen."* Oh, ***but God***, what a glorious phrase. He changes everything. God can be invited into the most desperate of circumstances, the most wretched of lives, the most hopeless of cases; and He changes it all.

Our call is to love God back, to pour out our hearts before Him and let Him fill our hearts with Himself. And in this, we can know that we are called to great purpose...His purpose.

No matter where you are in life right now, no matter what is happening or what you have done; there is a truth that can change it all...***but God***. Turn to Him, trust Him, trust His Son Jesus and let Him work all things together for good in your life. It won't happen overnight...it's a journey, it takes time. When we come to Him, He receives us, and we stand in His grace. Dearest ones, find your rest in Him this day.

Those Closed Doors and Welcome Mats

The Lord of hosts has sworn saying, "Surely, just as I have intended so it has happened, and just as I have planned so it will stand...For the Lord of hosts has planned, and who can frustrate it? And as for His stretched-out hand, who can turn it back?"

(Isaiah 14:24 and 27)

a poem: by carole l. Haines

I stood there, pondering; confused by what I saw.
The Door was locked before me,
a door I felt the Lord had led me to.
Locked, Bolted, Immovable.
Why would He lead me here, just to send me away again?
Then I looked down at my feet, no
Welcome Mat was found.
No place to wipe my worn and muddied feet.
It was such a long and arduous journey
through forests and fields,
along Stony paths and winding roads.
And all for what,
to lead me to A Door that would not open for me.
I turned in frustration, and began to walk away
when I noticed before me lying on the Ground

The Welcome Mat,
about a stone's throw away
to the right and slightly hidden.
This Path had not been traveled much
and needed to be cleared
Being a Gardener,
I began to clear away debris, weeds and brush until
The Welcome Mat was clearly visible
and the path revealed itself.
Was I to take it?
Follow this New Path into the Unknown,
Away from any Shelter and left exposed?
I took the chance to follow it,
forgetting all about the locked door
I was careful to stay on this New Path
Leaving crumbs so, If I needed to,
I could always find my way back.
The further down the Path I went,
the more I wanted to continue
For the Forest thinned,
with Sun penetrating the Understory of Trees
Light filtered in, Brighter and brighter,
more and more.
The Mud was drying as the Sunlight warmed it.
My cloak was drying.
My face now glowed as I broke through

into a field of Wildflowers
and still the path went on.
It was then I realized,
It is not A Destination that I truly seek
For it is the Journey that is Our Destination,
It is The Journey that we truly need
This Journey with Jesus is our Path.
"When one door closes, another opens,
but we often look so long and so regretfully upon
the closed door that we do not see the one that
has opened for us." (Alexander Graham Bell)

Like Father, Like Child

I have often heard it said that our children are constantly watching us. They see us when we don't know they are watching. They hear stories about us from those who have known us for a really long time. Some stories we may not be so proud of, but others have proven to be iconic for our children. Caleb had a story such as this. When Moses sent out twelve men into the land to spy it out, only two came back with positive reports, Joshua and Caleb. The other ten caused the people's hearts to fear so much that they chose not to move forward and receive the inheritance that God had promised them when they left their bondage in the land of Egypt. They spent forty years wandering around in that wilderness. So now fast forward forty years, and please read below from the book of Joshua. Moses has died and Joshua has been given the mantle of leadership by God to lead the people into the land of promise.

"Then the sons of Judah drew near to Joshua in Gilgal, and Caleb the son of Jephunneh the Kenizzite said to him, "You know the word which the Lord spoke to Moses the man of God concerning you and me in Kadesh-barnea. I was forty years old when Moses the

servant of the Lord sent me from Kadeshbarnea to spy out the land, and I brought word back to him as it was in my heart. Nevertheless my brethren who went up with me made the heart of the people melt with fear; but I followed the Lord my God fully. So Moses swore on that day, saying, "Surely the land on which your foot has trodden will be an inheritance to you and to your children forever, because you have followed the Lord my God fully." Now behold, the Lord has let me live, just as He spoke, these forty-five years, from the time that the Lord spoke this word to Moses, when Israel walked in the wilderness; and now behold, I am eighty-five years old today. I am still as strong today as I was in the day Moses sent me; as my strength was then, so my strength is now, for war and for going out and coming in. Now then, give me this mountain about which the Lord spoke on that day, for you heard on that day that Anakim were there, with great fortified cities; perhaps the Lord will be with me, and I will drive them out as the Lord has spoken. So Joshua blessed him and gave Hebron to Caleb the son of Jephunneh for an inheritance. Therefore, Hebron became the inheritance of Caleb the son of Jephunneh the Kenizzite until this day, because he followed the Lord God of Israel fully. Now the name of Hebron was formerly Kiriath-arba; for Arba was the greatest man among the Anakim. Then the land had rest from war. (Joshua 14:6–15, KJV).

And so Caleb comes to Joshua and asks for what God has promised him. Joshua blesses Caleb and grants his request. I am sure this story was iconic in the lives of Caleb's children. So Caleb's daughter, Achsah, was apprised of her father's bravery and faithfulness to God. So in a day and age where women were not given inheritances and portions of land, she had the boldness to step forward, like her dad, and make a request
(Joshua 15:13-19).
Caleb grants her request and gives her the upper and lower springs.

We most certainly do pass on a heritage to our children, our heritage of faithfulness and boldness. We pass on a legacy of perseverance and trust. *"Jesus said to them, 'My food is to do the will of Him who sent Me and to accomplish His work.'" (John 4:34).*

So, Lord Jesus, we desire to pass this legacy of faith to our children. We are imperfect parents who are growing up, in so many ways, right alongside our own kids.

But dearest God, grant the desires of our hearts, as parents, to pass on boldness and faithfulness, trust and perseverance. Lord, may our very food be to do Your will and to accomplish Your work. Lord, please bless us with passing this legacy onto each of our children. You make all things beautiful in Your time.

In Jesus's name, we pray. Amen.

Be a Blessing

When the Sabbath was over, Mary Magdalene, and Mary the mother of James, and Salome, bought spices, so that they might come and anoint Him. Very early on the first day of the week, they came to the tomb when the sun had risen. They were saying to one another, "Who will roll away the stone for us from the entrance of the tomb?" Looking up, they saw that the stone had been rolled away, although it was extremely large. Entering the tomb, they saw a young man sitting at the right, wearing a white robe; and they were amazed. And he said to them, "Do not be amazed; you are looking for Jesus the Nazarene, who has been crucified. He has risen; He is not here; behold, here is the place where they laid Him. But go, tell His disciples and Peter, 'He is going ahead of you to Galilee; there you will see Him, just as He told you.'" (Mark 16:1–7)

I love that these women had no idea how the stone was to be moved, but they went forward anyway. They intended to bless Jesus, but instead, they were witnesses to the greatest miracle to have ever occurred throughout history.

They waited until the Sabbath was over, and then they went and spent their own money to buy spices to anoint Jesus's body, to bless Him. Even as they were moving forward, they wondered how they would roll away the stone. They knew they were not strong enough, but they were determined to anoint the body of their beloved Jesus. God made a way even more wonderful than they could ever have imagined. I believe Jesus was blessed by this. For He knew they would be there, He knew they were coming to anoint Him. He sent a messenger there to declare the joyous truth that, “He is risen.” Their original purpose was never fulfilled; they were never able to anoint Jesus’s body, for He had risen. But God had an even bigger joy in store for these women who set out to be a blessing.

So don’t give up on a blessing; don’t fall short of a journey to do something good for someone else. It is not enough to plan it, think about it, and delight in it. We must give our blessings—legs, hands and feet. We must give our blessings our voice.

If God has placed it in your heart to go forward and bless another, do so, with all your heart. Things may not turn out the way we expect, but I believe God knows our hearts, and when we set out to bless others, we also will be blessed by God, perhaps in greater ways than we could ever possibly imagine. Keep blessing one another in Christ.

Now to Him who is able to do far more abundantly beyond all that we ask or think, according to the

power that works within us, to Him be the glory in the church and in Christ Jesus to all generations forever and ever. Amen. (Ephesians 3:20-21)

His Blood Be on Us

When Pilate saw that he could prevail nothing, but that rather a tumult was made, he took water, and washed his hands before the multitude, saying, I am innocent of the blood of this just person: see to it. Then answered all the people, and said, His blood be on us, and on our children." (Matt. 27:24-25)

These people were willing to be guilty of the blood of Jesus, guilty of putting Him to death. They called their innocent children into their own sin. Yet aren't we all really guilty of putting Jesus on that cross? We are all responsible for His death. These people get the blame a lot, but we are also guilty before our holy God.

"For all have sinned and fallen short of the Glory of God...and the wages of sin is death, but the gift of God is eternal life through Jesus Christ our Lord."
(Rom. 3:23; 6:23).

I find it amazing that they actually used the words, "His blood be upon us," because that is exactly what needs to happen in order for each of us to be saved. One of the most amazing books of the Bible is the book of Hebrews. It describes in detail just how perfectly Jesus fulfilled all of the requirements of the Law in order to purchase our freedom from sin.

But when Christ appeared as a high priest of the good things to come, He entered through the greater and more perfect tabernacle, not made with hands, that is to say, not of this creation; and not through the blood of goats and calves, but through His own blood, He entered the holy place once for all, having obtained eternal redemption. For if the blood of goats and bulls and the ashes of a heifer sprinkling those who have been defiled sanctify for the cleansing of the flesh, how much more will the blood of Christ, who through the eternal Spirit offered Himself without blemish to God, cleanse your conscience from dead works to serve the living God?
(Hebrews 9:11–13)

I've heard of churches that don't want to mention "the blood of Christ" anymore. Too shocking, too messy. But here is what God says about it: *How much severer punishments do you think he will deserve who has trampled under- foot the Son of God, and has regarded as unclean the blood of the covenant by which he was sanctified, and has insulted the Spirit of grace?* (Hebrews 10:29)

As believers, we must never be ashamed to talk about the Blood of Christ, it cost Him so much suffering to pour it out on the mercy seat of God in Heaven. We are saved because of His great sacrifice.

Let us cry out in a grateful and humble voice.

Lord Jesus, Your blood be on us, for we need You, dear Lord, we need to be cleansed by the sacrifice you made for us, by the shedding of your blood, once for all who would believe.

I believe, Lord Jesus, and I thank You for the precious gift of Your blood poured out for me, for us, for all who will look to You and cry out for mercy. Amen.

Perspective on the Journey

I was taken on an old familiar journey with God, Moses, and the people of Israel, as I read the Bible this morning. I will relate to you what God showed me as I read through this familiar true story of redemption. I have broken up the passage and interjected the insights God gave to me as I read. (All texts are taken from Exodus 14)

"They are wandering aimlessly in the land; the wilderness has shut them in. " (verse 3)

This was the perspective that pharaoh had of the people's rescue and travels with God. Pharaoh was used to victory, not defeat. He was used to getting his way all the time. He just couldn't understand how God had beaten him. He refused to bow, repent, and acknowledge that God alone is the Lord. God had come into the land of Egypt and demanded the release of His captive people.

Even after all the plagues God had brought and then miraculously removed from the land, Pharaoh refused to see the truth.

The world's perspective is never God's. We must constantly and persistently look at what God says and rest in Him. We are never wandering aimlessly with God, and no wilderness can shut us in. I personally have experienced God's deliverance from a wilderness time I thought would be the end of me. But He is our rescuer and guide.

"The Lord will fight for you while you keep silent." (Verse 14)

I was helpless in my own wilderness to effect change. I was hemmed in on every side and had nowhere to turn except to God in prayer. I was so afraid, even as the people of Israel must have been in their own captivity. I curled up, emotionally, spiritually, mentally, and even physically sometimes, and waited silently for God. I was either going to be overcome by my wilderness experience, or God was going to have to overcome it for me. He did. He fought for me, while I could do nothing but keep silent. He is a redeeming God.

Then the Lord said to Moses, "Why are you crying out to Me? Tell the sons of Israel to go forward. As for you, lift up your staff and stretch out your hand over the sea and divide it, and the sons of Israel shall go through the midst of the sea on dry land. (Verses 15-16)

All I wanted to do after my escape was to sit in my chair and stare out the windows at the trees. I felt safe, and didn't want to risk moving out again. But God was calling me out. He was calling me to move forward, to go ahead with what He was telling me to do. This ministry of writing ***Hisshadowings Devotions,*** is the beginning of that stepping out journey.

The angel of God, who had been going before the camp of Israel, moved and went behind them; and the pillar of cloud moved from before them and stood behind them. So it came between the camp of Egypt and the camp of Israel; and there was the cloud along with the darkness, yet it gave light at night. Thus the one did not come near the other all night. (Verses 19–20)

Even as God is leading us, He will come behind us and protect us. He will be our rear-guard. He will give us people who feel led to watch over us, encourage us, and spur us on. I have several of those now. I had really never had them before, and maybe never would have known that joy, had I not stepped forward in faith.

If I had remained in my chair, safe, warm, and staring out at my trees, I may never have known the security of the God who moves before me and stands behind me. I may have never known the God who gives me light in the darkness, so that no one comes near me to harm me, because He is my protector.

But the sons of Israel walked on dry land through the midst of the sea, and the waters were like a wall to them on their right hand and on their left. When Israel saw the great power which the Lord had used against the Egyptians, the people feared the Lord, and they believed in the Lord and in His servant Moses. (Verses 29-31).

God calls, we yield, we step out, we obey, and the rest is up to Him. I don't have the power to effect change, to awaken sleeping spirits, or to stir languishing faith; but if God wants to do that in and through me, just by doing what He says, so be it. He is the vine, I am a mere branch; if I remain in Him, I can bear much fruit. Apart from Him, I know I can do nothing. It's not about me, never has been, never will be.

Who is like You among the gods, O Lord? Who is like You, majestic in holiness, Awesome in praises, working wonders? (Exodus 15:11)

Obedience to His call, endurance in the hardest of times, resting in His care, will always lead to the praise and glory of God. Praise to God alone, from me, and all who see. Amen.

A New and Living Way

Therefore, brethren, since we have confidence to enter the holy place by the blood of Jesus, by a new and living way which He inaugurated for us through the veil, that is, His flesh, and since we have a great priest over the house of God, let us draw near with a sincere heart in full assurance of faith, having our hearts sprinkled clean from an evil conscience and our bodies washed with pure water. Let us hold fast the confession of our hope without wavering, for He who promised is faithful; and let us consider how to stimulate one another to love and good deeds, not forsaking our own assembling together, as is the habit of some, but encouraging one another; and all the more as you see the day drawing near.

(Hebrews 10:19–25)

I don't make New Year's resolutions anymore. I have made too many in the past and never kept any of them. By this time of year, most resolutions are broken. But we don't need human resolutions in order to change because we have a God who transforms us wholly and completely. God does deal with us all uniquely and individually.

God knows our weaknesses better than we do. He knows our every fear, our secret regrets. He knows that we get discouraged, depressed, and feel trapped sometimes.

The person I feel trapped by and want to get away from the most is myself. But instead, when I falter, I just need to open the Word of God. He speaks to me there and leads me back on the right path of sitting before God and listening to Him.

It's like crawling up into God's lap and letting Him tell me a story. His story of my life. It's like pouring out my heart before Him and listening as He speaks directly to my hurts, my fears, my needs, wants, and desires.

If all experienced God in the same way and responded to Him with identical worship, the song of the Church triumphant would have no symphony, it would be like an orchestra in which all the instruments played the same note.(C.S. Lewis, The Problem of Pain, United Kingdom: Centenary Press, 1940)

We are each a different instrument in God's orchestra, a different note in His song, a different part of His symphony. And we need to tell each other how God meets us in our everyday lives.

For myself, there is no greater joy than hearing how God is working in the life of another brother or sister in Christ. God loves each one of us so completely, that there is no competition for His attention, no jockeying for position. There is just sweet fellowship with God and with one another, as we sit at His feet, being all He has created us to be.

I have told people many times. If all I am called to do is cook and clean for my family, jot down a few words in this tiny little blog, and speak of His kindness to me, whenever I have opportunity; If this is all He has called me to, and I do it with all my heart, then God is just as pleased with me as he is with Billy Graham, or Beth Moore, Joyce Meyer, or Kay Arthur.

I don't need to be anybody big or well-known to be pleasing to God. I can almost guarantee you that these people did not envision big things for their lives, but it was what God called them to, and they have been faithful. I have been called to "smaller things, in smaller realms." May I do all that I do for the glory of God, and may he be pleased with me.

I pray that God will bless you this day, with a deeper knowledge of who He is, who you are, and just how precious and beautiful, just how perfect and complete His calling upon your life truly is.

May you sit before Him and listen, crawl up into His lap and be loved. May you be closer to God at the close of this day than you were when it began.

The Unfruitful Deeds of Darkness

I definitely had an “Aha” moment this morning. I am an early riser, usually sometime between 5:00-6:00 a.m. That’s just how my body clock works. I don’t want to get up that early, I just am—ping—awake that early. Well, this morning, I was up even earlier, about 1:30 a.m. I get a lot done at these hours, but I try to keep things very quiet, and do a lot in dim lighting in my room, as I do not want to wake my precious husband.

So, I’m fumbling around in dim lighting this morning, trying to find my lotion for my feet. I spot a container that looks just like it. I save my old containers and refill them, (growing up on a tight budget, I guess). Anyhow, the container I grabbed was not my lotion, but my “modge-podge.” In the dim lighting, I smeared it all over my feet, and couldn’t understand why I was having such a hard time getting my socks on.

What a mess! I had to wake my husband anyway so he could get me a wet wash cloth because I didn’t want to track my gluey feet all over the wood floors in our room.

Too funny, right! Even at 2:00 a.m. my husband was

still laughing at me, and so was I.

This is a humorous way to look at a very serious matter, the deeds that we do when no one else is around.

Do not participate in the unfruitful deeds of darkness, but instead even expose them; for it is disgraceful even to speak of the things which are done by them in secret. But all things become visible when they are exposed by the light, for everything that becomes visible is light. For this reason it says, "Awake, sleeper, and arise from the dead, And Christ will shine on you." Therefore be careful how you walk, not as unwise men but as wise, making the most of your time, because the days are evil. So then do not be foolish, but understand what the will of the Lord is. (Ephesians 5:11–17)

God loves me way too much to let me stay in my destructive patterns. I have been a believer a long time, but am still finding there is much work to do, much more room to continue growing and learning that "His ways are higher than my ways."

So, take heart, believer, whatever God has "put the finger on" in your life right now, whatever the "unfruitful deed of darkness," that You are struggling with, God can show you the way out. The first step is to agree with Him in confession about the sin. He only wants to free us from what is holding us back from fully walking with Him.

May His light shine bright in your darkness and show you the way in which you should walk. His love is perfecting love, encouraging love, never-ending love.

Yield yourself to the correcting love of God. It is a wonderful thing to be loved by someone who wants to build you up and lead you in ways that will make you beautiful, in His time.

God's Sure Guidance

For such is God, Our God forever and ever; He will guide us until death. (Psalm 48:14)
You, in Your great compassion, did not forsake them in the wilderness; The pillar of cloud did not leave them by day, to guide them on their way, Nor the pillar of fire by night, to light for them the way in which they were to go. (Nehemiah 9:19)
The Lord is my Shepherd, I shall not want. He makes me lie down in green pastures; He leads me beside quiet waters. He restores my soul; He guides me in the paths of righteousness for His name's sake. Even though I walk through the valley of the shadow of death, I fear no evil, for You are with me; Your rod and Your staff, they comfort me. You prepare a table before me in the presence of my enemies; You have anointed my head with oil; My cup overflows. Surely goodness and lovingkindness will follow me all the days of my life, And I will dwell in the house of the Lord forever. (Psalm. 23)

We just visited a foreign country for the first time a year ago. This one was thirteen hours away. The culture was so vastly different from my own. I would not have even considered venturing out without an escort or a guide. I believe there were dangers there for us that we never even knew about. We felt like we were divinely protected through the whole thing, carried so to speak.

I know our leaders protected us, and God kept us safe through them. They didn't tell us the dangers, moment by moment, but we knew they were there. Our leaders had a way of escape set up for us, should the unforeseen occur. This world can feel a bit like that for us as believers.

It is a world littered with pitfalls, uncertainties, doubts, fears, and unknowns. I need to lean so intensely on God's guidance, as I navigate unfamiliar pathways. I love God for His unchangeableness, His constancy.He is our security. I can rest easy in the day and at night only because I know Him as the one who holds my future in His hands.
God is never fickle, like people so often are. God is simply God, and I love that about Him. He forever stays the same.

Thank You, Father, for Your unceasing, radically tenacious love. I need it, and I am so very grateful for it.

The Lord Was My Stay

He sent from on high, He took me; He drew me out of many waters. He delivered me from my strong enemy, And from those who hated me, for they were too mighty for me. They confronted me on the day of my calamity, But the Lord was my stay. He brought me forth also into a broad place; He rescued me, because He delighted in me. (Psalm 18:16-19)

Oh, to be rescued by God. What a wondrous thing it is. It's actually quite romantic. I know that sounds corny, but those of you who have been in places of utter and complete desperation surely know what I mean. God is my knight in shining armor, rushing in on a mounted steed and swooping me up in His arms and carrying me away from harm.

I have lived this truth and am so thankful for the experience. The scariest thing about it all was that I found myself in a place of utter helplessness. I used to be a radical control freak. I tried to keep everyone safe, everything safe.

My journey began in a blizzard. My husband was trying to drive home from work in a blizzard. The commute normally took one hour; this day, it would take four. Now, this was before cell phones, so I waited in tears, wringing my hands, afraid he was out on the road somewhere, cold and stranded. When he finally came home, I nearly knocked him over with a hug.

In my worrying, I had practically convinced myself that he was dead. This was just the beginning of a long journey out of my controlling tendencies and into resting in God's Sovereignty.

Each step of the way, I found myself in more and more difficult situations that were completely out of my control. The greatest of these situations was so devastating, I felt I would never recover from such losses. Yet God has done exceedingly abundantly beyond all that I could ask, thing or dare to imagine. (Ephesians 3:20)

God is so faithful to His promises, so true to His Word.

He truly has never left me, nor forsaken me, just as He promised.

He will never leave or forsake any of His children. Only He can deliver us from evil. Come to Him with your greatest fears and begin that journey today. He will walk you through it and never, ever give up.

He who began a good work in you will be faithful to complete it to the end. (Philippians 1:6)

Trust Him with your greatest fears, and watch Him

walk with you right out of them, even if it's a long journey, like mine. Come to Him, and you will find that He is forever faithful.

We Will Tell

We will not hide them from our descendants; we will tell the next generation the praiseworthy deeds of the Lord, His power and all the wonders He has done for us." (Psalm 78:4)

When we were kids, being "told on" was a very bad thing. But we have a God who wants to be told on. He wants us to say, "God, I'm going to tell on you!" We need to tell our children, and their children. They need to hear the wonderful things God is doing in the lives of His people.

I love to listen to stories of how He leads others to Himself. God is so resourceful. I recently heard of a woman who was led to share with a complete stranger in a bagel shop.

People love personal stories. We all have them. Stories of how God brought us out a tricky situation, how He corrected us when we were going astray. We have stories of restoration, stories of healings, stories of hope, stories of peace that passes understanding. We can sit in the midst of chaos and still have His peace.

We may not feel able to go and knock on the doors of strangers to share Christ, but we can pray for opportunities to tell our stories. We can share what

God has done for us to a world that feels God is dead.

So let's tell our stories to each other, to our coworkers, to all the world. God wants to be "told on," so let's do Him the honor. Let us be those lights of hope to others, wherever God has placed us.

His Wonders

It has seemed good to me to declare the signs and wonders which the Most High God has done for me. (Daniel 4:2)

God works so magnificently in our lives. He is the *"God, who gives life to the dead and calls into being that which does not exist."* (Romans 4:17). I have recently been led to study this word, wonders, in the Bible. Here is part of the definition: *"that which, for its extraordinary character, is apt to be observed and kept in the memory."*

We have all had God do things in our lives that seem to defy explanation, something extraordinary. But God's wonders can also be found in the everyday things. I have watched a mother fox play with her two young kits right in my own backyard.

I have seen sunsets that seem to set the sky on fire. But I think some of the most extraordinary wonders are simply found in obedience to the things that God has shown me to do.

I would be confused about what to do in a certain situation. I would come to God's Word and ask Him to give me guidance. He would speak to me from His Word, I would begin to practice what He

showed me, and it
works.

One of my favorite Bible studies is "Experiencing God" by Henry Blackaby. Here is a quote about obedience from that study.

"Obedience is the outward expression of your love for God. The reward for obedience and love is that He will reveal Himself to you. If you have an obedience problem, then you have a love problem. God is love, His will is always best. God is all knowing, His directions are always right. God is all-powerful, He can enable you to do His will. If you love Him, you will obey Him. When you come to a moment of truth when you must choose whether to obey God, you cannot obey Him unless you believe and trust Him. You cannot believe and trust Him unless you love Him. You cannot love Him unless you know Him."

I myself have come to believe that God's wonders are often linked to obedience in what He asks. Moses had to step forward into that sea in order for it to part. Peter had to get out of the boat in order to walk on the water.

Lord Jesus, work your wonders in and through us in both ordinary and extraordinary ways. May we be a light that shines your love to this world. May we be guideposts, pointing many to You, so you can work Your wonders in their lives too.

That One Branch

by: Carole L. Haines

Strolling in the field, beside the wooded place
a single limb was jutting out and hanging in my
face tempted, at first, to break it off,
I reach, but then draw back
remembering a time that will soon come,
when I will want to have that one branch,
that single limb, and the little cones it bears
For a celebration beckons me from a future time
reminding me of how I've used these branches
to celebrate in kind
So I leave it grow and watch it sway,
on this windy Autumn Day
until a Winter's chill reminds me
to seek it where it sways
For its glorious smell, its vibrant green,
its cones of little seeds come into my house
and decorate a Holy Nativity scene.
Its fragrance fills my home with joy
and reminders that I too,
am to be a fragrance of my Lord
all the long year through,
Its vibrant green reminds me
of the life I have within

placed there by the Love of God,
who came to die for me
Its cones of seeds beckon me
to reach out with that grace
and share the love of my dear Christ
in every single place.
And so that one branch, that single limb,
to many it may seem justin the way,
or perhaps, a mere inconvenience
but to me, it's a reminder
of all my Christ has done for me.
And so we, too, can view ourselves
as an awkward little branch
perhaps we feel, we're not much use,
in this world so grand and vast
but God delights to confound the arrogant
by using little branches that no one would suspect
and so I wait and grow and bloom,
for one day, my God will reach down from His heav-
en
and use me to love, encourage, and teach
and I will decorate the world with His love,
as that pine branch did for me

For consider your calling, brethren, that there were not many wise according to the flesh, not many mighty, not many noble; but God has chosen the foolish things of the world to shame the wise, and God has chosen the weak things of the world to shame the things which are strong, and the base things of the world and the despised God has chosen, the things that are not, so that He may nullify the things that are, so that no man may boast before God. (1 Corinthians 1:26–29)

God-ipulated/Used By God

We live in a society where it's deemed to be a bad thing to be "used." We want to make sure we are not being taken advantage of, used, or manipulated. What does that word even mean, manipulated?

Manipulate- *to control or play upon by artful, unfair, or insidious means especially to one's own advantage.* (Merriam Webster Dictionary)

Wow! I truly don't want to be "manipulated!" But can we create a new Word here? How about Godipulated? Yes, Godipulated. That's what I want to be, used by God in a wonderful plan. I want to be used by God to be a blessing to others. I have learned so much from God, so many freeing things that I am bursting to share.

I learn so much from the Body of Christ too. There was one precious soul yesterday who said the coolest thing in class. She shared how grateful she was to God for the fact that she is the happiest she has ever been in her whole life. This young lady is over sixty and it blessed me to hear her say that.

I was given a surprise birthday party by my mom and sister this past Friday, and in one of the cards, someone wrote, "The 2nd 50 years are the hardest."

How depressing. I'd much rather go with the mind-set of the woman above.

When asked about her happiness she said, "Oh, there's a story to the glory!" We all could tell from that statement, she had been through a lot of hard stuff in her life. But look at the glory she gives God, despite the hard times. How marvelous.

Therefore everyone who hears these words of Mine and acts on them, may be compared to a wise man who built his house on the rock. And the rain fell, and the floods came, and the winds blew and slammed against that house; and yet it did not fall, for it had been founded on the rock. Everyone who hears these words of Mine and does not act on them, will be like a foolish man who built his house on the sand. The rain fell, and the floods came, and the winds blew and slammed against that house; and it fell—and great was its fall. When Jesus had finished these words, the crowds were amazed at His teaching; for He was teaching them as one having authority, and not as their scribes. (Matthew 7:24-28)

Oh, yes God, use us up. Godipulate us to be a blessing to others. There truly is a story to the glory. What's yours? Let God use it!

One

I look at what divides the Church today, and I mourn. For the petty things that divide us are as nothing compared to our glorious Lord and Savior, Jesus Christ, who unites us.

And He put all things in subjection under His feet, and gave Him as head over all things to the church. (Ephesians 1:22)
But speaking the truth in love, we are to grow up in all aspects into Him who is the head, even Christ, and one Spirit. (Ephesians 4:15)
For all who are being led by the Spirit of God, these are sons of God. just as also you were called in one hope of your calling. (Romans 8:14)
Now may the God of hope fill you with all joy and peace in believing, so that you will abound in hope by the power of the Holy Spirit. (Romans 15:13)
Therefore, we have been buried with Him through baptism into death, so that as Christ was raised from the dead through the glory of the Father, so we too might walk in newness of life. (Romans 6:4)

I look at these verses, and it makes me wonder why it is so hard for us, as believers, to dwell in unity. We have so much in common. Our differences can be corrected as we each choose to go back to the simplicity of "purity and devotion to Jesus Christ." (2 Corinthians 11:3)

Father God, help us to lay aside our differences, and go back to the source. Guide us to run back to Your Word daily and choose what it says over tradition or doctrinal statements. Teach us to go back to Jesus, in the Garden of Gethsemane, and die with Him there to our own thoughts, ideas, and preconceived notions.

Help us to cry out in that same Garden, "Not my will be done, Lord, but yours."

In Jesus's holy name, amen.

Of Two Minds

I would never have considered myself a two-faced person, deliberately saying one thing to someone, and then talking about them behind their backs. Yet, I am sure I have done this in my life, as we all have. However God showed me that in some areas, I am of two minds.

I must learn to discern what is true, what is not, and what I simply cannot know.

It is this place of "not knowing" that causes the most problems for me. If I don't know something, my own opinions slip in there at times, masquerading as the truth. It is easy for me to become deceived by my own opinions.

I believe this is what God is trying to show me right now. The only remedy for my own opinions is Truth. And truth is only ever found in God and His Word.

For the Word of God is Living and active, sharper than any two-edged sword; piercing even to the dividing of soul and spirit, and of joints and marrow, and is able to judge the thoughts and intentions of the heart. (Hebrews 4:12)

I am learning to die to my own opinions about things, and instead, to *"take every thought captive and make it obey Christ."* (2 Corinthians 10:5).

I am learning to let go of my own opinions . I am learning to trust God to set my Standard of Truth. He is the One who *works all things together for the good of those who love Him* (Romans 8:28).

It's a lifelong journey, but in the end, I will be free from being of two minds on issues. I will only have the mind of Christ, for eternity. I look forward to that reality.

But in the meantime, I humbly submit my tired, broken, and often "wrong-opinionated," self to God.

*"He who promised is faithful to complete the work He has begun in me." (*Philippians 1:6).

Thank You, God, for loving me, for loving all of us, this much. Amen.

A Tapestry of Amazing Beauty

I have been on vacation for over a week. Just got back two days ago. It's so great to get away, but I am very appreciative of having a home to come back to. Home is a place to call my own, a place where I belong.

The hope of heaven is like that. Not a place to come back to, but the assurance of a home in heaven for me. One of the things that my husband and I were looking forward to when we got back home was going back to our church. We are in such a precious and beautiful part of the Body of Christ.

Yesterday's worship time was so sweet and nourishing, like a cool glass of lemonade on a very hot day. We just drank it in and bathed in the kindness of our fellow believers in Christ.

When I returned home, I needed to tend to my now overgrown garden. In the sweltering ninety-seven degree heat, some of my flowers had flourished and some had faded away. There were a few in particular that had grown so tall, they were now top heavy and tipped over.

I gently tucked them back into the midst of the other flowers. Their stems gave them support and allowed them to be seen in all their splendor.

That is what the Body of Christ is supposed to be. We are tucked into the midst of people who support us, and whom we support. There, together, we bloom well and glorify our King and Savior in all our different colors, shapes, and fragrances.

There is nothing more beautiful than a wildflower garden. All the colors blend into a tapestry of amazing beauty. The precious Body of Christ is to be like that as well, a tapestry of amazing beauty. *"Behold how good and how pleasant it is for brethren (believers) to dwell together in unity."* (Psalm 133:1).

Clamoring for the Bottom Rung

God promises that the work He has begun in me
He will complete it, He will perfect it.
He promises that all things will work together
for my good, and His Glory.
That He is writing in me a wonderful story
of things lost that are found.
Of things broken that are made whole again.
Things dirtied and soiled made white as snow.
Blind men will open their eyes to see.
The deaf hear words and songs and sounds
The lame leap up and dances around.
Fools are made wise in the Kingdom of God
The last shall be first and the first shall come down,
and all the houses are built on Solid Ground.
People will be clamoring for the bottom rung
Instead of climbing and clawing their way to the top.
The Kingdom of God is upside down.
Where the smallest seed is the most precious found
And we lose all we have to gain what is best.
Sitting at His feet is where we find true rest.
Where once more, all that can be shaken, will be
so that only what God gives is left to see
A Kingdom that cannot be bought or sold,

A Kingdom inside us that never grows old
A Kingdom unshakable, strong, and free,
where all is redeemed and finally made right
Until then, I sit here and sing songs long sung,
and wait my turn, clamoring for the bottom rung

“For God sees not as man sees, for man looks at the outward appearance, but the Lord looks at the heart.” (1 Samuel 16:7).

At His Gate

"Now there was a rich man, and he habitually dressed in purple and fine linen, enjoying himself in splendor every day. And a poor man named Lazarus was laid at his gate, covered with sores, and longing to be fed from the scraps which fell from the rich man's table; not only that, the dogs also were coming and licking his sores.(Luke 16:19-21)

This morning, as I spent time with Jesus, I began to think about who is lying just outside my gate covered in sores. Now I don't mean literally lying outside, or even literal sores; but rather, who is near to me, around me, who is hurting?

Precious Lord Jesus, Make us aware of the hurts of others around us. In America, most of us have plenty compared to so many in the rest of the world. Yet I know that You, Jesus, love each person in the world. There is no partiality with you, no favoritism. You once said that to whom much is given, much will be expected. *(Luke 12:48)*

Lord, you have given us so much in this great country. Help us to be generous to those outside our gate.

You told us in the story of the good Samaritan that

whoever is in need, he is our neighbor.
So all who have needs that we can meet are our Lazarus. Guide us to see as you see, hear as you hear, and be your hands, your mouth, your feet, and your provision for others.

Forgive me for how much I keep back for myself. Give me a generous heart, a heart like yours, a heart of compassion and mercy. Give me a generous spirit and the means to help others. In Jesus's name, Amen.

A Guidepost

And he (John the baptist) looked at Jesus as He walked, and said, "Behold the Lamb of God!" The two disciples (of John) heard him speak, and they followed Jesus. Jesus looked around and saw them following and asked them, "What do you seek? They replied, 'Rabbi, where are You staying." Jesus answered them, "Come and See!"
(John 1:36-39)

Jesus, I pray I will have this kind of impact on people. May they hear me speak, "Behold the Lamb of God," and may they turn and follow You, Jesus. I see in this passage a pattern for discipleship:

1. I look to Jesus as He walks in His Word and in my life.

2. I declare to others, "Behold the Lamb of God."

3. They will hear Jesus for themselves and follow Him.

4. Jesus will ask them what they seek.

5. He will invite them to come and see.

6. They will follow and stay with Jesus.

If I stand and point and speak of this wonderful Savior I have, then I have done well. If I light a lamp to illuminate the way for others to walk by how much I love , I have done well. If I ask forgiveness when I am wrong, admit my faults and failings so others will see that I know I need a Savior, then I have done well.

Keep it simple, dear believer. Be that lampstand, that guidepost, that beacon shining in a dark world, pointing the way to the Savior who loves them.

Before the World Was

"Blessed be the God and Father of our Lord Jesus Christ, who has blessed us with every spiritual blessing in the heavenly places in Christ, just as He chose us in Him before the foundation of the world, that we would be holy and blameless before Him. In love, He predestined us to adoption as sons and daughters through Jesus Christ to Himself, according to the good pleasure of His will, to the praise of the glory of His grace, with which He favored us in the Beloved." (Ephesians 1:3-6)

God had already set aside His own Son, Jesus, and the whole plan of salvation.When Jesus was forming Adam out of clay, and when He reached inside and pulled out a rib to form Eve, He knew we would rebel. He knew the whole human race would fall into darkness and separation from God. Jesus knew that we would never be able to live up to God's perfect standard in order to save ourselves. Christ knew all this and chose to create us anyway, so great was His love for us.

It reminds me of the brave women who have been told that if they carry their baby to term in the womb, it will kill them. Out of love for their unborn child, they disregard their own lives and risk their lives to carry that child and give them a chance to live.

Jesus laid down His life to carry us into the salvation that only He could give.

Please take the time to read all of Ephesians 1 today and bask in the beautiful marvel of God's incredible love.

Waiting in Jerusalem

And this is Life Eternal, that they might Know Thee, the Only True God, and Jesus Christ whom You have sent.
(John 17:3)

I'm waiting in Jerusalem for power from on high.
So Weary and bothered by the question "Why?"
I'm waiting in Jerusalem for the Holy Spirit
to descend on me and pour
Take hold of my life, Lord, a living sacrifice
a Song, a fragrant offering
my joyous heart will spring
while I'm waiting in Jerusalem
We serve a God not bound by time and space
Our bodies, His temple. Our hearts, His Holy place!
Bought by the Blood of His Amazing Grace
We rejoice to serve Him thankfully
while we wait And yearn to see Him face-to-face
with heavenly footsteps in an earthly place
I'm waiting in Jerusalem for power from on high
By: Carole L. Haines

God promises He will give us all we need as we wait for Him. He promises that there is nothing

we will ever face that He will not give us the power to overcome. He is truly a faithful God. Let us wait upon Him in our times of need, as the disciples did after the Resurrection. Jesus told them to wait in Jerusalem, for power from on High.
(Luke 24:29).
So let us wait for Him, and He will surely empower us to overcome and do His will.

An Anchor for the Soul

Sometimes life can open up a torrent like floodwaters crashing through, sweeping away all sense of security or constancy. We find ourselves clinging for life to whatever we can grab onto. Perhaps we find ourselves washed downstream, holding on to what used to be the roof of our home, What we thought was our safe haven.

Life can be like that. That phone call in the middle of the night, that knock at the door, continues to send shivers up my spine to this day, even years later. Anxiety paints pictures of worst-case scenarios in our minds. It creates rivers of weariness, and we try to paddle upstream against its raging torrents.

One of the hardest truths to come to grips with, is just how little control we have over our own lives. When the cold winds of change begin to blow, weariness just wraps around me like a blanket. I could never hold up to all the pressure life hurls at me, if I didn't have God to hold on to. I know God's in control and He holds my life tenderly in His Hands.

But I just wonder how much I, myself, can take. When fear and anxiety hit, I try to get in the boat of God's Word and remind myself of His truth.

"Therefore we who have fled to God for refuge can have confidence as we hold to the hope that lies before us. This hope is a strong and trustworthy anchor for our souls. It leads us through the curtain into God's Inner Sanctuary. Jesus has already gone in there for us.
(Hebrews 6:18-20, NLV)

God's hope is an anchor for our souls. Our circumstances, bodies, relationships, etc. will all be changing, nothing is constant except God.
I think I was trying to hold onto things that were incredibly transient. When I hold onto God and His promise, I am at peace within, even when everything outside of me is swirling out of control. I just learn to go deeper into the realms of the soul, God's inner sanctuary, the only source of true hope.

Learned Obedience

Although He (Jesus) was a Son, He learned obedience through the things which He suffered. (Hebrews 5:8)

If Jesus learned obedience through suffering, I should have known that was how I would need to learn it. The challenge is learning to receive God's correction as an act of love. For a long time, I was the center of my universe. I thought the world revolved around me and my happiness, or lack of it.

When I went through my darkest times of correction, I thought God was angry at me. Then I figured He must not love me anymore. And, in course, I thought he was punishing me for all the bad things I did.

But having held on to Christ through it all, I learned the painful way of God's love.

It's so easy to receive His encouragement, but when He has to sharpen us through correction a bit, well, we don't like that very much. But like any good parent, discipline comes as an act of love.

God does love to lavish good gifts upon His children, but one of His most misunderstood gifts is the gift of His correction; His reproof, His training in righteousness.

"All Scripture is God-breathed, and profitable for teaching, reproof, correction and training in righteousness." (2 Timothy 3:16)

It's so wonderful to search the Word of God and be taught by it. Such wonder and beauty is found there. But there are three other purposes for His Word listed in the above passage of Scripture. Reproof, correction, and training in righteousness. I have learned my most cherished lessons through God's loving on me in these three ways. It's just a fact that most of us seem to learn best from our mistakes and not our triumphs. At least, this is true for me.

All discipline for the moment seems not to be joyful, but sorrowful; yet to those who have been trained by it, afterwards it yields the peaceful fruit of righteousness. (Hebrews 12:11)

God disciplines us because He loves us. He always disciplines us for our good. And once we have been trained by His discipline, it yields the peaceful fruit of righteousness. Want peace? Then embrace God's loving discipline.

He has loved me into a new woman, and He's not finished yet. I love His encouragement , but I've grown to love His discipline as well.

Thank You, God, for being a great Father, and loving me too much to let me have my own way. Amen.

Grace and Truth Were Realized

And the Word became flesh, and dwelt among us, and we saw His glory, glory as of the only begotten from the Father, full of grace and truth. John testified about Him and cried out, saying, "This was He of whom I said, 'He who comes after me has a higher rank than I, for He existed before me.'" For of His fullness we have all received, and grace upon grace. For the Law was given through Moses; grace and truth were realized through Jesus Christ. No one has seen God at any time; the only begotten God who is in the bosom of the Father, He has explained Him." (John 1:14-18)

The Word of God is so amazing. It informs us, reveals to us so much. I could study it every day, all day long, all my life, and never exhaust its riches. One of the true gems that God showed me in His Word is found right here in John 1.

Have you ever wondered why the God of the Old Testament seems so different from the God of the New Testament? Well, I have. The Law was given by God through Moses, and when we understand that the Law was basically given to teach us that we could never be righteous on our own, it makes more sense. The Law is a constant reminder of our inability to live perfectly holy lives.

The Apostle Paul tells us that, *"Therefore the law was our schoolmaster to bring us to Christ, that we might be justified by faith. But after the faith is come, we are no longer under a schoolmaster."* (Galatians 4:24-25).

The Law was our Schoolmaster used to bring us to Christ? How, by revealing in us our sinful ways and our need of a Savior.

I was scared of the Old Testament God when I was growing up. But that's what it's like to experience God outside of grace, outside of Christ. The Old Testament God is the same God, but in the New Testament, He is *God made flesh, come down to dwell among us* through Christ. I have never been afraid of Jesus.

I now see that I was afraid of the Old Testament God because it's like approaching God with no clothes on, completely naked. But in Christ, we are wrapped in His own robe of righteousness and brought before God, hand in hand with Jesus.

Grace and truth were never realized until they were realized through Jesus Christ. What a precious and awesome God we serve.

Transparency

I've noticed, as I ride along through the winter woods, just how easy it is to see everything. Things are hidden by all the green growth in springtime and summer. Autumn yields a splendor all its own. But winter exposes all the imperfections that were hidden all year long. People dump things in the forests sometimes, like old tires or debris. It's easy for those things to be overlooked when summer growth hides them. But in the winter, things are stripped down to the bark, to the barebones. Everything gets exposed.

I think I am in a winter in my own life. God is exposing those hidden things He wants to deal with. He's let them be revealed so He can touch those places and heal them. He wants to clean up the mess inside me, so that in the spring, new life will not be covering old things, dead things, discarded things. He wants to truly make all things new.

Then the eyes of both of them were opened, and they knew that they were naked; and they sewed fig leaves together and made themselves loin coverings. We need this time of transparency, this time of exposure. Adam and Eve tried to sew fig leaves together to hide their nakedness. (Genesis

3:7)

They had sinned by disobeying, and they didn't want God to know it. God teaches us to run toward Him when we have sinned, not follow the natural inclination to run away from Him.

For the Word of God is living and active. It is sharper than any two-edged sword cutting between soul and spirit, joint and marrow, It exposes the thoughts and desires of the heart. Nothing in all creation is hidden from God. Everything is naked and exposed before His eye, and He is the one to whom we are accountable. (Hebrews 4:12-13)

Adam and Eve fled from God's presence and tried to cover up their sin and disobedience. But in verses 14-16 of Hebrews 4, we are shown just how much we need to ignore our natural inclination to run from God when exposed, and instead to come boldly to Him.

So then, since we have a great High priest who has entered Heaven, Jesus, the Son of God, let us hold firmly to what we believe. This High Priest of ours understands our weaknesses, for He faced all the same testings we do, yet He did not sin. So let us come boldly to the throne of our Gracious God. There we will find His mercy, and we will find

grace to help us when we need it most.
(Hebrews 4:14–16)

So when God brings us into a winter season, where a lot of hidden things are exposed, let us resist the urge to run and hide, as Adam and Eve did. Let us instead run to our great high priest, Jesus, and He promises to show us mercy and grace, just when we feel we need it most.

Sliver of Glass

As the mist settles like a Bridal Veil upon the Thirsty
Land
And the morning light breaks across the sky,
we meander hand in hand
Reminiscing of times we shared,
the laughter, tears, and pain
How we've lived the age-old tale
of nothing ventured, nothing gained
We're Seeing life through a sliver of glass
Where the light reflects and the rainbows dance
Where we gaze together through Smoky glass
Sharing glimpses of the road ahead
and shadows of the life we've had
Fragile as a fresh spun web
soaked in drops of morning dew
Clinging to the towering cliffs
where harsh winds are howling through
Our lives are bridging chasms
in Shadow lands of Misty Blue
Where hope surprises us with joyful sounds
of laughter between us two
We're Seeing life through a sliver of glass
Where the light reflects and the rainbows dance.
Where we gaze together through Smoky glass

Sharing glimpses of the road ahead,
and shadows of the life we've had
As the dust settles from our lives.
When what's lost is found and tears are dried
Our dreams are often realized;
less in the here and now, more in the by and by.

Come now, you who say, "Today or tomorrow we will go to such and such a city, and spend a year there and engage in business and make a profit." Yet you do not know what your life will be like tomorrow. You are just a vapor that appears for a little while and then vanishes away. Instead, you ought to say, "If the Lord wills, we will live and also do this or that (James 4:13-16).

Stand Out

A winter landscape is stunning in so many ways. Snow-scapes take your breath away with their purity. Waking up to the sun shining through a world veiled in ice, every blade of grass, every branch and leaf covered and sparkling.

But one of the subtler beauties of winter is the lone sycamore tree, standing amidst the dozens and dozens of dark-brown hues and colors of other trees. They stand like cathedrals in the middle of a crowded city, like castles on a cliff, a lighthouse in a storm. God's Word reveals this little gem of a Scripture in The Gospel of Matthew.

"*You are the light of the world. A city set on a hill cannot be hidden; nor does anyone light a lamp and put it under a basket, but on the lampstand, and it gives light to all who are in the house. Let your light shine in such a way that they may see your good works and glorify Your Father in Heaven.*" (Matthew 5:16).

We are lights, whether we want to be or not, simply by the fact that we are followers of

Jesus. People are watching us, sizing us up to see how we measure up to the faith we proclaim.

Our transparency, honesty and humility are key elements of this transformation process the World is watching. Notice that I underlined the phrase,

"in such a way!"

We must seek to be transparent in our motives in all we do, seeking purity of heart and mind. Letting our lights shine for God's Glory not our own. There is a delicate balance to be kept.

If our lights are shining before men and they glorify God, we are being those beacons in the night, those cathedrals in the city, those lights in the darkness. We are those tall white sycamore trees adorning the winter landscape; drawing people to the very hope that still draws us deeper and deeper into Christ.

We Advertised in Heaven and They Came

A few years ago, I was a part of a team of more than twenty people who went to a foreign land to share Christ. Our pastor had been given a vision from God of the worship team doing a big outreach concert in this country to reach people for Christ. We are a part of a small church. No one had heard of us outside of our own community.

But God had called, given a vision, and we answered the call. I fought against going. I gave all sorts of reasons, but God kept knocking at the door of my heart, and I finally yielded. We ran into problems in getting my passport and visa. I kept saying, "I guess I'm not supposed to go!"

Those who had gone to this country before, kept encouraging me that this was the enemy's work.
So, I plodded on, carried by their faith, not my own. The task was arduous, thank the local pastors of this country, who arranged so much. I witnessed our own Leadership Team walking on invisible steps, in the air of faith. They just kept moving out, believing everything would be as God would have it.

They never wavered.

We visited many villages, most of them remote. I have never experienced such precious people in my entire life. I was simply amazed at their faith and joy in the midst of great poverty and opposition. I was so humbled and realized that God would not let me stay home because He knew these people would forever change my life and how I viewed the world.

The day before the concert, the stage hadn't been built yet, there was so much left to do. But faithful men spent almost a straight twenty-four hours getting it done—both our men and the locals. The day of the concert arrived, and I heard concerns and whispers of whether it would actually take place. Would people even come? Were there enough posters up and handouts given?

So many were praying, both at home and in this foreign land. Two hours before the concert, a woman arrived with her baby. She handed the baby to one of our women and asked us to care for it. She was going to commit suicide, she said, because she had a demon.

People ran and got our pastor, and he came and prayed for her. He cast the demon out in Jesus's name and led this beautiful woman to Christ. Her baby was then handed back to her. That was to be the beginning of many miracles we would see that night.

You see, we had prayed, and God responded. At home, they were praying and fasting. Here, in this land far away, the local believers were praying, and God heard. All the advertising in the world can't do what God can do.

We had advertised in Heaven...and they came. He drew People to Himself. We were expecting maybe a little over two thousand, but God had prepared more hearts.

It was an outside venue, so they were sitting on the walls of the courtyard. They were standing on the tops of city buildings. Not to see us, but to come to know this God who had led us there. To hear about Jesus and His love, His hope, His Message of Redemption.

The final count was over eight thousand. Over two thousand came forward to receive Christ as their Savior and Lord. We came and we gave our meager gifts, like the boy with five loaves and two fish,which Jesus Blessed, and fed five thousand with that small gift (Mark 6:38).

Yes, we prayed. We advertised in Heaven, through prayer, and God reached the hearts of thousands.

One thing I learned is that people are hungry for the love of God, for the salvation only He can offer, and we are called to share it. Prayer is our advertising in Heaven. It is us crying out for God to reach hearts, heal bodies, change lives. And only He can. I will never see prayer the same way again. Our God is an awesome God, and I am so thankful for His will and goodness.

Reminiscing Beyond the Lies

I actually slept in a bit today, 6:30 a.m. Amazingly wonderful thing, this "sleeping in." I went out to the kitchen to begin cooking one of the two Thanksgiving turkeys.

I am hosting at my house this year, and I want to make sure there is enough meat for everyone, so I am doing a backup bird. I put in one of my old familiar favorite CDs and began singing, trying to harmonize, and just generally enjoying one of my favorite songwriters of all time. My mind seemed to pick up more and more of the actual lyrics, as if I had never heard them before.

I began to feel that this beloved songwriter may actually be kind of lost, lonely, and still searching for meaning in life. I listened as each song went by, picking up words like: chaos and void, traveler, final truth, beyond the lies. I pondered these words, these concepts, and realized just how blessed I am to have found the truth beyond the lies. Or should I say, the Truth found me.

*Jesus *said to him, "I am the way, and the truth, and the life; no one comes to the Father but through Me.*
(John 14:6)

Jesus found me, I received Him, and He promised me, All that the Father gives Me will come to Me, and the one who comes to Me I will certainly not cast out.
(John 6:37)

I trust in Him. I believe Him. Thus began the Greatest Journey of my Life. You see, I remember what it felt like to just be hanging out there, detached from my Creator. He made me for a special purpose. I was a starry-eyed dreamer when I was young. I knew what I wanted to be, and always assumed it would just happen. But it didn't, and nothing worth having just "happens." God allowed some severe difficulties to pop up in my life, and I, like the Apostle Paul, pleaded with the Lord to take these things away.

So to keep me from becoming conceited because of the surpassing greatness of the revelations, a thorn was given me in the flesh, a messenger of Satan to harass me, to keep me from becoming conceited. Three times I pleaded with the Lord about this, that it should leave me. But he said to me, "My grace is sufficient for you, for my power is made perfect in weakness." Therefore I will boast all the more gladly of my weaknesses, so that the power of Christ may rest upon me. (2 Corinthians 12:7-9)

God did not remove my difficulties, these thorns in my flesh. God left them in my life so that in overcoming them, I would become strong in the Word of God, strong in character and devotion, strong in love and gratitude toward Him. Notice that Paul says twice that the reason God left this thorn in his flesh was to *keep him from becoming conceited.*

I believe that these thorns in each of our lives are very necessary. We all start out as someone who needs to grow into the callings God has on our lives.

In the days of His flesh, He offered up both prayers and supplications with loud crying and tears to the One able to save Him from death, and He was heard because of His piety. Although He was a Son, He learned obedience from the things which He suffered. (Hebrews 5:7-8)

If Jesus learned obedience from the things which He suffered, how much more must we?

O, God of glory, Your mercy knows no measure, Your grace has no bounds, and Your love is completely unfathomable. How I long to bask in Your eternal presence. But until you call me home, help me to point others to You, so that they may be found by You as well, and be delivered from the loneliness, the sense of detachment, the emptiness and void of a life spent without You, the Creator and lover of their souls.

Thank You, God, for joining me today in reminiscing beyond the lies. Thank You for leading me to Jesus; the Way, the Truth, and the Life. I give you each moment of this day, and every day for the rest of my life.
In Jesus's name and love...Amen!

Come Now, Let Us Reason Together

Just sitting awhile with God is a very precious privilege, bought at a very high price. We didn't pay the cost, Jesus did. God knew we couldn't save ourselves, so He came to earth as an infant.This is one of the most treasured, yet confounding truths of the Word of God. God's love for mankind goes beyond the scope of our ability to comprehend, to understand. It must just be received with an attitude of humility and gratefulness. God is ever-reaching out to us, His beloved creation, His treasured ones. Here is what He says to His people in The Book of Isaiah:

"Come now, and let us reason together," says the Lord, "Though your sins are as scarlet, They will be as white as snow; Though they are red like crimson, They will be like wool. "If you consent and obey, You will eat the best of the land; "But if you refuse and rebel, You will be devoured by the sword." Truly, the mouth of the Lord has spoken.

(Isaiah 1:18-19)

The word reason in this context means: to argue, convince, prove to be right; to convict, to rebuke or correct.

All discipline for the moment seems not to be joyful, but sorrowful; yet to those who have been trained by it, afterwards it yields the peaceful fruit of righteousness. Therefore, strengthen the hands that are weak and the knees that are feeble, and make straight paths for your feet, so that the limb which is lame may not be put out of joint, but rather be healed. (Hebrews 12:11-13)

One of the greatest and most wonderful privileges in belonging to God through Jesus Christ in the privilege of being corrected, guided, and led by the Spirit of God. Led out of our old and harmful ways of thinking, and into God's wholesome truth. This word, reason, is used fifteen times in the book of Job. No one in all the Bible had more right to consider himself justified in arguing with God than Job.

But God ultimately corrected Job's understanding of personal suffering with these words.

Then the Lord said to Job, "Will the faultfinder contend with the Almighty? Let him who reproves God answer it." Then Job answered the Lord and said, "Behold, I am insignificant; what can I reply to You? I lay my hand on my mouth. Once I have spoken, and I will not answer; Even twice, and I will add nothing more." (Job 40:2-5)

There are times we see deep into the character of God; His love, His mercy, His genuine concern for the welfare of those He loves. THis Vision usually comes after the Suffering, not before. When we see this, we gladly yield to the guidance of such a Heavenly Father. I have been disciplined severely by God in my short lifetime, and I can tell you that God truly disciplines those He loves. He cares deeply for us, as any good parent would for his or her own child. He cares too deeply to let us wander off into dangerous and destructive decisions.
I am forever grateful for God's discipline of love. He has rescued and saved me countless times. There are sorrows and hardships I have had to endure, but I know there must be countless others that I have been able to avoid because I yielded to God's voice as He corrected me. Yield to the love of God's correction. How happy you will be in the end.

You have dealt well with Your servant, O Lord, according to Your word. Teach me good discernment and knowledge, For I believe in Your command-

ments. Before I was afflicted I went astray, But now I keep Your word. You are good and do good; Teach me Your statutes.

(Psalm 119:65)

This, I Pray

Sometimes, I just don't know how to pray for people and their situations. I mean, truly, sometimes, I don't even know how to pray for my own family members because their issues are deeper than I can see.

But I always take comfort in knowing that God knows just how deep the rabbit-hole goes in the lives of those I love and care for. When I just don't know how to pray, these two prayers from Ephesians enable me to pray God's blessings and His will over those I am praying for. This, I pray:

That the God of our Lord Jesus Christ, the Father of glory, may give to you a spirit of wisdom and of revelation in the knowledge of Him. I pray that the eyes of your heart may be enlightened, so that you will know what is the hope of His calling, what are the riches of the glory of His inheritance in the saints, and what is the surpassing greatness of His power toward us who believe.

(Ephesians 1:17-19)

For this reason I bow my knees before the Father, from whom every family in heaven and on earth derives its name, that He would grant you, according to the riches of His glory, to be strengthened with power through His Spirit in the inner man, so that Christ may dwell in your hearts through faith; and that you, being rooted and grounded in love, may be able to comprehend with all the saints what is the breadth and length and height and depth, and to know the love of Christ which surpasses knowledge, that you may be filled up to all the fullness of God. Now to Him who is able to do far more abundantly beyond all that we ask or think, according to the power that works within us, to Him be the glory in the church and in Christ Jesus to all generations forever and ever. Amen. (Ephesians 3:14-21)

Scripture is filled with these prayers, especially in Psalms. So when you don't know how to pray, don't not pray. Let's pray the Scriptures all over our loved ones. We can never go wrong in praying God's Word.

References

All scripture quotations, unless otherwise indicated, are taken from the New American Standard Bible®, Copyright © 1960, 1962, 1963, 1968, 1971, 1972, 1973, 1975, 1977, 1995 by The Lockman Foundation. Used by permission.

Scripture quotations marked (kjv) are taken from the Holy Bible, King James Version, Cambridge, 1769. Used by permission. All rights reserved.

Scripture quotations marked (nlt) are taken from the Holy Bible, New Living Translation, copyright © 1996. Used by permission of Tyndale House Publishers, Inc., Wheaton, Illinois 60189. All rights reserved.

More - Just for You!

Carole and her husband Bruce make beautiful music together, and they've compiled some of their favorites in the list below for just for you! You can **access these songs within the INSPIRE U APP** simply by **scanning the code below** or by following the links to Soundcloud.

Download the free: **InSpireU App**

Join to access even more Inspirational Works

Input This Special **Unlock Code: 800008**

https://soundcloud.com/hisshadowings/back-to-bethlehem

https://soundcloud.com/hisshadowings/a-single-word

https://soundcloud.com/hisshadowings/come-to-the-table

https://soundcloud.com/hisshadowings/signs-of-life

https://soundcloud.com/hisshadowings/eden-reclaimed

https://soundcloud.com/hisshadowings/stand

https://soundcloud.com/hisshadowings/bread-of-life

https://soundcloud.com/hisshadowings/listening-to-god

https://soundcloud.com/hisshadowings/this-treasure-mine

https://soundcloud.com/hisshadowings/go-before-me

https://soundcloud.com/hisshadowings/line-in-the-sand

https://soundcloud.com/hisshadowings/catbird

https://soundcloud.com/hisshadowings/heaven-sure-sounds-wonderful

https://soundcloud.com/hisshadowings/glory-to-glory

Watch for The Next Books In This Series

About the Author

Carole has battled anxiety and depression most of her life. She was finally diagnosed with Social Anxiety Disorder in her twenties. Her struggle for normalcy drove her to seek and dwell in God's Word for truth, wisdom, and comfort.

Carole began writing her blog, *hisshadowings.com*, over 10 years ago. She has written over 750 Devotions, as well as various Poems and Songs. She seeks simplicity as a lifestyle... Her simplicity? Finding the most important thing to spend your life doing and doing that one thing. Her relationship with God, through Jesus Christ, is that One Thing.

She is a Trained and Certified Chaplain. She and her husband of 35 years are Leaders in their local Celebrate Recovery Chapter. She is an Author, Minstrel, Poet and Artist.

When she is not writing, she is out and about on Nature photography trips with her husband, Bruce, and will often paint one of the pictures taken on those excursions. They enjoy life together beneath 40-foot Weeping Pines, surrounded by lots of rescued, furry friends.

About The Publisher

Founded in 2014, by Diane K. Bell, Legacy Lane Publishing focuses on helping new and emerging writers. Ideal clients are heart-centered Christian- principled authors with a sacred message.

Don't get caught in the self-publishing maze. Take advantage of professional guidance, and marketing expertise. Our clients delight in becoming #1 Best Selling Authors, and discovering today's most effective book marketing techniques. You will always control pricing and keep 100% of your royalties.

For more information contact:
https://LegacyLanePublishing.com
Phone: 303-242-4461

Made in the USA
Monee, IL
24 August 2022